NATIONAL HEALTH INSURANCE IN ONTARIO
The Effects of a Policy of Cost Control

William S. Comanor

American Enterprise Institute for Public Policy Research
Washington, D.C.

William S. Comanor is professor of economics at the University of California at Santa Barbara. On leave from this position, he currently serves as the director of the Bureau of Economics at the Federal Trade Commission.

Distributed to the Trade by National Book Network, 15200 NBN Way, Blue Ridge Summit, PA 17214. To order call toll free 1-800-462-6420 or 1-717-794-3800. For all other inquiries please contact the AEI Press, 1150 Seventeenth Street, N.W., Washington, D.C. 20036 or call 1-800-862-5801.

Library of Congress Cataloging in Publication Data

Comanor, William S.
　　National health insurance in Ontario.

　　(AEI studies ; 276)
　　Includes bibliographical references.
　　1. Insurance, Health—Ontario. I. Title. II. Series: American Enterprise Institute for Public Policy Research. AEI studies ; 276.
HD7102.C2C65　　　368.4'2'009713　　　80-11129
ISBN 978-0-8447-3379-1

AEI studies 276

© 1980 by the American Enterprise Institute for Public Policy Research, Washington, D.C. All rights reserved. No part of this publication may be used or reproduced in any manner whatsoever without permission in writing from the American Enterprise Institute except in the case of brief quotations embodied in news articles, critical articles, or reviews. The views expressed in the publications of the American Enterprise Institute are those of the authors and do not necessarily reflect the views of the staff, advisory panels, officers, or trustees of AEI.

"American Enterprise Institute" and　⬚　are registered service marks of the American Enterprise Institute for Public Policy Research.

CONTENTS

PREFACE

A country such as the United States of America which is now considering [government funding of health services] has a tremendous opportunity to learn from what has happened in other countries. I hope that they will regard the developments in Canada as an experiment from which they can learn lessons that will allow them to avoid some of the problems we have created for ourselves.
(J. Fraser Mustard, dean of the Faculty of Medicine of McMaster University and chairman, Ontario Ministry of Health Task Force on Health Planning, 1973–1975)[1]

This project originated during the academic year 1974–1975, which I spent at the Department of Economics of the University of Western Ontario in London, Ontario, Canada. In that department, which provided a focus on Canadian economic issues, there was considerable discussion of public policy dealing with the Ontario health care system. After complete national health insurance was adopted throughout Canada, health care costs grew rapidly. As a result, direct restraints were proposed on the supply both of physicians and of hospital beds throughout the province. This project began as an attempt to examine the economic implications of these proposals, the need for them, and their likely implications.

This study was originally supported by the Ontario Economic

---

[1] J. Fraser Mustard, "Towards an Understanding of the Health Delivery Concept," in J. Alex Murray, ed., *Health Care Delivery Systems in North America: The Changing Concepts* (Windsor, Ontario: Canadian-American Seminar, University of Windsor, 1977), p. 24.

Council, an agency of the provincial government. With its help, extensive data were collected on the health care system in Ontario. I am indebted to the council for its financial support and to various sections of the Ministry of Health in Ontario for access to unpublished, as well as to published, data.

Most of the research on this project was carried out at the University of California, Santa Barbara, a lively and energetic research environment. I am grateful to my colleagues there for their willingness to discuss this study, particularly to H. E. Frech for his many helpful comments and suggestions, and also to John Marshall and to Llad Phillips for useful discussions with me. Valuable comments were received as well from Robert G. Evans, Martin S. Feldstein, Victor R. Fuchs, Peter Ruderman, and Alan Wolfson.

This manuscript was substantially completed by September 1978, when I became director of the Bureau of Economics at the Federal Trade Commission. The manuscript was revised and edited on my own time during the two years after I joined the staff of the commission. The views are, of course, my own and not necessarily those of the Federal Trade Commission, nor of any individual commissioner.

Especially during the latter stages of this research, I received much encouragement and support from Robert Helms of the American Enterprise Institute. Dr. Helms permitted me to complete this manuscript at a slow pace, which was determined largely by the energy I had left after completing my duties at the Federal Trade Commission. I would also like to thank Susan Khoury of AEI for typing the manuscript and final revisions.

The debate over adoption of national health insurance in the United States has appeared at various times in the past and will surely do so again in the future. Whatever the benefits from these proposals, there are costs as well. I believe it necessary to examine the Canadian experience with national health insurance before proceeding with a major realignment of the health care system in the United States. By reporting the Ontario experience, my aim is to contribute to the ongoing debate over this major policy issue.

1

Introduction

It has commonly been stated that the United States is twenty years behind Canada in its policies toward health care.[1] This statement suggests that there is much the United States could learn from studying the Canadian experience with government-provided health insurance. Although no single program prevails throughout Canada, separate plans of government-financed medical care were enacted in each of the Canadian provinces in response to the federal government's offer to bear a large portion of the cost. In this study, we will examine the Ontario Health Insurance Plan and consider the implications of the Ontario experience for public policy in the United States.

The Ontario plan was designed to maintain the existing structure of the medical profession. An essential feature of the plan was its retention of a fee-for-service payment mechanism. The major change was payment by the government for the services provided; medical care would be supplied as before, but the bill would be sent to the government rather than to the patient.

When the plan was introduced, on October 1, 1969, physicians were permitted to bill the province for 90 percent of the existing fee schedule of the Ontario Medical Association (OMA) and their patients for the rest. In 1971, however, the additional billing was prohibited.

---

[1] See, for example, Spyros Andreopoulos, "The Health of Canadians," in Spyros Andreopoulos, ed., *National Health Insurance: Can We Learn from Canada?* (New York: Wiley, 1975), p.6.

If a physician submitted a bill to the government, he could not bill his patients as well. In effect, the OMA schedule of fees less 10 percent became the approved basis for reimbursement.

The program of national health insurance, or Medicare, was superimposed on the hospital insurance plan, which had been introduced ten years earlier on January 1, 1959. In April 1972, the two programs were amalgamated into the Ontario Health Insurance Plan. In this plan, hospital care is not reimbursed according to the services provided to individual patients, but rather by means of overall budgets supported by the Health Insurance Plan. Charges for nonapproved services, however, such as private or semi-private accommodations, are billed directly to the patient. Although the reimbursement mechanism is indirect, the quantity of services supplied still provides the basis for government payment through its influence on hospital budgets.

A major objective was universality of coverage, which has been substantially obtained. Nearly all physicians practicing in Ontario have belonged to the Health Insurance Plan, although an increasing number of medical specialists have "opted out" in recent years. Coverage includes approximately 98 percent of the population. Although compulsory premiums are charged to the working population, these cover less than a fourth of the total cost. These premiums are reduced for low-income groups and fully eliminated for those on public assistance and for those over sixty-five years of age. In effect, a specific tax is levied to pay for medical services that does not cover the full costs of the program: general tax revenues are required to make up the difference. In regard to both hospital and physician services, financial constraints have been removed from the patient population and the cost placed directly on the government agency administering the health care plan. While part of the required expenditures are paid from premiums and part reimbursed by the Canadian government, what remains must be paid from general provincial revenues.[2]

As Robert Evans points out, the essential justification for this system was "the naive medical-technical view of disease conditions arising independently in the population, requiring necessary care as defined by medical technology, generating costs again according to a fairly well-defined production technology and price structure."[3] Who pays for medical care, according to this view, is relevant only

---

[2] A more extensive discussion of the health care system throughout Canada is given in Maurice Leclair, "The Canadian Health Care System," in ibid., pp. 11–93. See also Jean-Luc Migue and Gerard Belander, *The Price of Health* (Toronto: Macmillan, 1974).
[3] Robert G. Evans, "Beyond the Medical Marketplace: Expenditures, Utilization and Pricing of Insured Health in Canada," in Andreopoulos, ed., *National Health Insurance*, p. 133.

2

for its effect on the distribution of income between the sick and the well, but the method of payment can have no impact on the quantity of care demanded or obtained. The demand for medical services was considered perfectly inelastic at the level of care required by medical considerations, and it was assumed there would be no difficulty in determining the amount of care required for various illnesses. As has become apparent, however, *these assumptions are inconsistent with actual experience.*

In 1975, the government of Ontario adopted a new set of policies. Restrictions were placed on the number of physicians permitted to enter practice in Ontario and on the number of hospitals beds in service. These measures were combined with the existing structure of the medical care system. Indeed, it is these additional measures that serve as the impetus for this study. Why were they considered necessary? What impact are they likely to have? More important, what do they indicate about the original program of health insurance in Ontario? This study is an attempt to provide some tentative answers to these questions.

Chapter 2 is an analysis of the effect of national health insurance on the market for medical services. The focus is on both the supply and the demand characteristics of the relevant markets as well as on the policy measures adopted. The aim is to examine the costs and benefits of the program of supply restraint.

The policy measures designed to reduce the quantity of services were directed at both physicians and hospital beds. Implicit in this approach was the assumption of a positive relationship between services used and the supplies of physicians and beds. An analysis of this relationship is therefore essential to determine the usefulness of the new policy measures. If, for example, the quantity of services that physicians wish to supply exceeds the quantity demanded, a change in the former may have little effect on the volume of services actually provided. Chapter 3 provides empirical estimates of these relationships.

The final chapter reviews the pattern of policy making toward health care in Ontario with the aim of determining the links between the policy decisions made in 1975, when restraints were instituted, and those made earlier, when national health insurance was first adopted. Underlying policy issues are considered, as well as the implications of this experience for the United States.

While there are many differences between the United States and the province of Ontario, there are sufficient similarities so that the problems faced in Canada may be anticipated in this country as well. By carefully examining the experience there, we can illuminate discussions of health care policy in the United States.

3

2

The Impact of Limiting Supply

This chapter presents a conceptual analysis of the effects of limiting the supply of physicians and of hospital beds. We examine the impact on consumers (or patients), on producers (or physicians and other providers of medical care), and on society. While the primary object of a policy of supply restraint was to reduce the cost to the Ontario government of the medical care system, there was inevitably a reduction in utilization as well. In the analysis below, we consider the costs and benefits of these actions within the current structure of the medical care system in Ontario.

The impact of a decline in expenditures on medical care can be divided into three elements. First, any reduction in the supply of services will force consumers to change their patterns of use. Patients will not receive as many services as they did previously, which will lead to some loss in utility. Second, there is a loss in utility to physicians who are prevented from practicing in Ontario, which includes both pecuniary and nonpecuniary components. Third, there are the prospective net savings to society from such actions, which are the difference between the savings in government expenditures and the perceived losses by consumers and producers.

The Role of Consumer Valuations

There are two distinct ways to evaluate the impact of medical care. Both have validity and importance. They are: (1) the demand by consumers for these services, as influenced by the advice of their physicians; and (2) the improvement in public health that results from medical care. To an extent, the first follows from the second, but the link is weaker than might be expected.

There are wide differences between the two. In the first place, the demand for medical services may derive from personal needs other than that of combating illness. Victor Fuchs distinguishes between "curing" and "caring" in terms of what is provided by physicians. To a large extent, he suggests, the demand for medical services is more a demand for the latter than for the former.[1] The effects of medical services on disease remission or on improved health is a different matter and may indeed involve only a small portion of the services consumed.[2]

It is sometimes argued that one or the other of these goals is paramount. To some observers, it is questionable whether consumer valuations have any relevance for policy, since medical care is a matter of public concern. Policies, it is said, should be designed to maximize the health of all citizens without regard to these valuations.

Evans suggests that the entire structure of Canadian health care policy represents an explicit rejection of the importance of consumer valuations. "In Canada, a political consensus has emerged which holds that health care, while not free to society, should be free to the individual. This may be exposed as an ethical principle that 'health is a right' to which citizens should have equal access regardless of economic circumstances."[3] In this setting, what is necessary is that adequate care be provided, where this standard is set by the physician rather than the patient. He continues, "Technical judgments of 'need' become more important guides to social policy than the revealed 'preferences' of uninformed consumers."[4]

Ontario policy, as stated by a recent minister of health, is generally consistent with this view: "The doctor's responsibility is to see that the amount of time as well as the degree, type and expense of the treatment he or she initiates should be kept at the level that the

[1] Victor R. Fuchs, *Who Shall Live?* (New York: Basic Books, Inc., 1974), pp. 64–67.
[2] Fuchs quotes approvingly from a letter by an American physician: "Fully 80 percent of illness is functional and can be effectively treated by a talented healer who displays work, interest and compassion regardless of whether he has finished grammar school. Another 10 percent of illness is wholly incurable. That leaves only 10 percent in which scientific medicine—at considerable cost—has any value at all." Ibid., p. 64.
[3] Robert G. Evans and Maurice F. Williamson, *Extending Canadian Health Insurance* (Toronto: University of Toronto Press, 1978), p. 3.
[4] Robert G. Evans, "Does Canada Have Too Many Doctors?—Two Views," *Canadian Public Policy*, vol. 3 (Summer 1977), p. 370.

consensus of professional judgment sees as necessary—and *must not be governed by the patient's demands.*"[5]

For the most part, health planners are concerned with the promotion of "health." Improved health would seem to be the ultimate objective from the point of view of consumers as well. Mark Pauly, however, argues differently:

> But thinking in terms of "health" is really misleading. There is no way to measure health or even define it. Some suggested definitions are so broad as to almost encompass the whole economic problem of welfare maximization in health maximization. Even if one could measure an individual's health, how are the healths of different individuals to be combined to obtain a measure of the "health of the nation"?
>
> Finally, even if health could be measured and combined for individuals, it is not clear, with a given batch of resources to be used for medical care, why the appropriate goal would be to maximize health in the usual sense in which it is measured by mortality and morbidity. People may be willing to trade-off additional bed-disability days or increases in the probability of death against the use of medical resources in a way which is more pleasing to them, which provides them with more satisfaction, or which satisfies other goals they may have. At the margin, personalized medical care or enjoyment of creature comforts may be more important than health. Sometimes it may be reasonable to inquire about the effect on health of a given expenditure, but maximization of health makes sense as a universally acceptable goal in all situations only when it is identified with well being or (perhaps) satisfaction, and then the notion is not distinct enough to be useful. Government planners may want to maximize "health" but there is no basic reason why they should want to do so.[6]

In contrast to the earlier position that consumer valuations should play no role in determining policy, Pauly's position is that consumer valuations should be the predominant factor. And consumer valuations of medical services and facilities may depend as much, or more, on the satisfaction they provide as on their effect on overall health.

Society generally provides support for specific goods and services because of the benefits that it will gain from their use, in addition to the benefits that will be gained by individual consumers. Thus, it is argued that society benefits from the recognition that all individuals have sufficient care available to them. Precisely because such values

---

[5] Frank S. Miller, "Remarks" (Toronto, February 2, 1976), p. 16 (emphasis added).
[6] Mark V. Pauly, *Medical Care at Public Expense* (New York: Praeger, 1971), pp. 6–7.

are widely held, public policies are adopted to assure that these services are available to all.

While the presence of interdependent utilities serves as a further rationale for existing Canadian policy, it disguises the important question of how many services should be provided and at what cost. While it is easy to suggest that all persons should have complete medical care available to them, it is far more difficult to determine how much care is appropriate and how much society should pay to provide it. Indeed, it is precisely this issue that underlies the current concern in Ontario regarding the supply of physicians and hospital beds.

Whatever importance we assign to consumer valuations, they are clearly relevant in the formation of public policy because they provide a standard by which to evaluate policy options. It is therefore necessary to consider the implications of consumer valuations before making policy decisions, even if our final conclusions differ from those suggested by that standard.

The Demand for Medical Services

In this analysis, medical care is aggregated into a single commodity, which is viewed alternately as physician and as hospital services. Martin Feldstein suggests that the demand for medical services rests on an incomplete agency relationship.[7] After the patient consults with his physician, the patient's preferences determine the demand for medical services, but these decisions are based on incomplete information. The physician adds not only his expertise in interpreting and acting upon these preferences but also, Feldstein suggests, "his own self-interest, the pressures from his professional colleagues, [and] a sense of medical ethics."[8]

That patients depend on their physicians for advice as to what medical services are required is incontrovertible. Similarly, there is no doubt that physicians dispense information along with medical services, and that this information influences consumer demands. These observations by themselves, however, are not sufficient to support an *incomplete* agency relationship, for they are equally consistent with a *complete* agency relationship. In the latter case, physicians act totally as their patients would have them act, adding only

---

[7] Martin S. Feldstein, "Econometric Studies of Health Economics," in M.D. Intriligator and D. Kendrick, eds., *Frontiers of Quantitative Economics II* (Amsterdam: North Holland, 1974).
[8] Ibid., p. 383.

their knowledge and expertise. Their actions are characterized as purely professional.

In a recent paper, Pauly defines a demand curve for medical services that is based on "fully accurate information."[9] Presumably this demand curve does not require omniscience, but rather represents the level of demand that would exist had patients the knowledge and information available to their physicians. On this basis, a complete agency demand schedule might represent the preferences for medical services that would exist when physicians and their families require care.

There is sparse evidence available on the relation between demand schedules based on complete agency relationships and those based on incomplete ones. The most direct information, which is, however, only suggestive, deals with the utilization of surgical services in California.[10] This study compares operation rates of certain standard procedures for physicians and their spouses with those reported by ministers, lawyers, and businessmen, together with their spouses. These groups were chosen to represent similar income and socioeconomic classes. From the data collected, the authors report: "Contrary to our expectations, we have found that the amount of surgical care received by physicians and their spouses is as high or higher than that for other professional groups and, on the average, higher than for the country as a whole."[11] While much of the cost of those procedures for the nonphysician groups is probably covered by health insurance, physicians may still face a lower effective price. On this account, a larger quantity would be expected. For these particular services, however, there does not appear to be a large difference between the demands of physicians and of nonphysicians of similar incomes and socioeconomic classes, and the agency relationship appears fairly complete.

Another study of this issue concerned physicians in British Columbia.[12] If the demand for medical services were exogenous and not subject to demand generation by physicians, "a 1 percent increase in physician stock (per capita) should lead to a 1 percent decrease in

[9] Mark V. Pauly, "The Role of Demand Creation in the Provision of Health Services," unpublished paper presented at meetings of American Economic Association, Dallas, Texas, December 30, 1975, p. 14.

[10] John P. Bunker and Bryan W. Brown, "The Physician-Patient as an Informed Consumer of Surgical Services," *New England Journal of Medicine,* vol. 290 (May 9, 1974), pp. 1051–55.

[11] Ibid., p. 1053.

[12] Robert G. Evans, E.M.A. Parish, and Floyd Sully, "Medical Productivity, Scale Effects, and Demand Generation," *Canadian Journal of Economics,* vol. 6 (August 1973), pp. 376–93.

workload and gross receipts per physician," with the total volume of physician services per capita remaining unchanged.[13] To test this null hypothesis, an empirical analysis was carried out. The authors found that the elasticity of total services provided in response to a change in the number of physicians is about 0.85, rather than zero.[14] Thus, the supply of physicians has a substantial impact on the volume of health care services provided.

The authors suggest that this finding is due largely to the effect of physicians on the demand for their own services. They admit, however, that two alternative explanations are also consistent with these empirical observations. The first is that there is substantial excess demand, or "unmet need," for medical services; the second, that an increased supply of physicians reduces the time cost to consumers for receiving care, resulting in increased demand.[15] Their findings are therefore not conclusive.

If the agency relationship existing between patients and consumers were complete, demand would be represented by Pauly's "fully accurate information" demand schedule. To the extent, however, that additional factors related to physician utility intrude, the agency relationship becomes incomplete and overall demand will increase with a greater number of physicians. Pauly argues that when prices are higher, physicians can be expected to increase their income by encouraging the consumption of more services, so that the demand schedule shifts upward and to the right.[16] What exists therefore is an entire family of demand schedules where the distances between schedules depend on the degree of incompleteness in the agency relationship.

In most studies of government actions, consumer benefits are measured by the consumer surplus gained or lost. As is well known, if we ignore income effects due to changes in tax rates necessary to finance the medical care system, these valuations are measured by the area under conventional demand schedules.[17] This usage, however, requires that demand conditions be exogenous, which is not so to the extent that agency relationships are incomplete. In such circumstances, it is sometimes argued that the concept of consumer surplus is too imprecise to be a proper tool for policy decisions.

---

[13] Ibid., p. 389.
[14] Ibid., p. 392.
[15] Ibid., pp. 392–93.
[16] Pauly, "The Role of Demand Creation," p. 15.
[17] For some examples of this type of analysis in matters of health policy, see Martin S. Feldstein, "The Welfare Loss of Excess Health Insurance," *Journal of Political Economy*, vol. 81 (March 1973), pp. 266–69; and Pauly, *Medical Care at Public Expense*.

A response to this charge is that policy judgments be founded on a hypothetical complete agency demand schedule. Pauly maintains that the optimal volume of medical services is indicated by the intersection of the demand schedule based on fully accurate information and the marginal social opportunity cost of those services.[18] Even though physicians may have a direct impact on actual consumption decisions, one can still define a welfare optimum founded on underlying consumer preferences.

A consumer's demand for medical services is also contingent on his state of health, so that aggregate demand is the sum of the contingent demands of all consumers. Because the state of health is uncertain, consumers typically wish to insure against conditions that would lead to a high demand for services. The optimal quantity, therefore, rests on an overall demand for services obtained where insurance is available.

The appropriate insurance for optimality is one where claims are defined by states of health rather than by medical services received. So long as these states are exogenous to the individual, wealth transfers take the form of lump-sum payments and appropriate incentives are maintained. The gains from risk spreading are achieved, and consumers continue to face prices that reflect the marginal costs of these services. The demand conditions that would exist under this form of ideal insurance determine the optimal quantity of health services, and it is the corresponding demand schedule which is given in figure 1 below.

The existing program of national health insurance departs from this ideal, since claims are paid in terms of services provided as influenced by the actions of consumers. Compared with an ideal insurance plan, this program leads to increased demand for medical services because it costs less to obtain additional services at any of the contingent states of health. Under the current program, those who become ill are afterward more wealthy than they would be with the hypothetical insurance plan. As a result, they demand more of most goods and services, including health care. Actual demands for medical services therefore lie to the right of the demand schedule used to define the optimal quantity of medical services.[19] For this reason as well, the demand schedule drawn in figure 1 lies below the actual quantity of services demanded.

There is a further issue to be faced in using this approach to

[18] Pauly, "The Role of Demand Creation," p. 27.
[19] For a related discussion, see Richard Zeckhauser, "Medical Insurance: A Case Study of the Tradeoff between Risk Spreading and Appropriate Incentives," *Journal of Economic Theory*, vol. 2 (March 1970), pp. 10–26.

FIGURE 1

THE SUPPLY AND DEMAND OF MEDICAL SERVICES

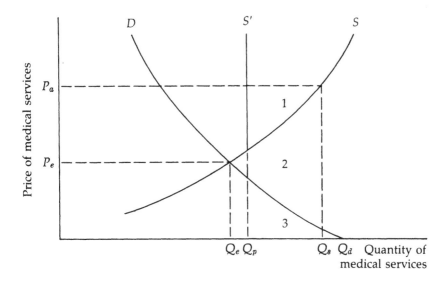

evaluate policy measures. This application of demand schedules pre-
sumes that those services with the lowest values to consumers, as
measured by the amount they are willing to spend for them, are
eliminated in order as total quantity is reduced. This occurs necessarily when services are allocated by price. Since a nonprice system
is used for medical services in Ontario, we need to consider whether
and how our evaluations are influenced by this factor.

Since medical services may not be available in sufficient quantities
to all who demand them, there must operate an implicit rationing
system. This system rests on the decisions of both physicians and
patients. Not only do physicians determine which patients are seen
first, presumably according to the seriousness of the symptoms presented, but also patients who are persistent in their attempts to receive medical care are more likely to do so. Since substantial time
outlays may be involved in obtaining both physician and hospital
services, patients who are most willing to bear these costs will generally receive the most services. When a queue exists, consumers
most willing to wait are those likely to receive the largest volume of
services.

11

To the extent that time costs are substantial, it seems likely that medical services will be rationed by the strength of consumer preferences. Those who want the services most will bear the high time costs required, while those whose preferences are weaker are unwilling to make the necessary effort. In addition, those to whom time is more valuable are also unwilling to bear the higher time costs. In the analysis below, we assume that rationing is carried out in accordance with consumer preferences, so that those consumers with the highest valuation of these services obtain them first, those with lower demand prices receive them next, and so on. Those with minimal demand prices—those to whom medical services are worth least in terms of the time they are willing to spend waiting to be served—are thereby excluded. In other words, we assume that rationing proceeds as though it were done by price.

This assumption may lead us to overstate or to understate the gains from a policy of supply restriction. When the supply of services is reduced, in the case of inefficient rationing, there is no reason to believe that consumers with the lowest demand prices are eliminated first from the market. If relatively more consumers with high demand prices are dropped, the actual consumer surplus forgone is larger than would be indicated in a conventional analysis, and the net gains from this policy are overstated. On the other hand, if relatively more consumers with low demand prices are foreclosed, net policy gains are understated.

The Supply of Medical Services

The supply of physician services includes two relevant dimensions, if we ignore inputs other than physician time in the production process. The first is the supply of services from a fixed number of physicians, and the second is the number of physicians who practice in Ontario. Turning first to the supply response of individual physicians, Feldstein suggests that individual supply schedules are backward-bending, in that lower real wage rates call forth an increased volume of services to maintain income levels.[20] Frank Sloan takes an opposite position. He contends that "there is a low degree of responsiveness of physician supply to wages and that the evidence to support a backward-bending supply curve . . . must be considered weak at

[20] Martin S. Feldstein, "The Rising Price of Physicians' Services," *Review of Economics and Statistics*, vol. 52 (May 1970), p. 130.

best."[21] In the analysis below, we do not resolve those differences but assume only that individual supply schedules are relatively inelastic.

The supply of physician services is also determined by the number of physicians. This number increased by 28 percent between 1970–1971 and 1975–1976, despite a decline in average real earnings. Although nominal earnings increased by 33 percent over this period, consumer prices in Ontario rose even faster—by 39 percent. Average earnings for physicians in 1975–1976 were $49,596, however, which apparently was sufficiently high to attract practitioners to Ontario.[22]

The aggregate supply schedule is the composite of these two elements. Whatever the elasticity of the average supply function of individual physicians, the supply of new physicians has responded strongly to the level of, if not to the change in, average earnings. In the analysis below, we assume a positive relationship between price and the supply of physician services.

The supply of hospital services presents a different picture. The number of aggregate patient-days was approximately constant during a recent five-year period. The 14.6 million patient-days supplied in 1974–1975 and 1975–1976 was unchanged from 1970–1971. At the same time, unit costs in terms of expenditures per patient-day have jumped by 107 percent, from $54 in the early year to an estimated figure of $112 for 1975–1976.[23]

Most of this increase in unit costs went to support substantially higher wage rates, which increased during this period by about 96 percent. There were also small increases in the volume of labor employed and in nonlabor inputs.[24]

As suggested by Joseph Newhouse, hospital administrators see their mission in terms of caring for the sick.[25] In their view, the more care that can be provided, the better. They view their objective as the maximization of the volume of services provided, subject to a constraint imposed by their financial resources. Higher levels of government support, which exceed increased wage payments, are likely to be associated with larger quantities of services provided. Even with a constant volume of patient-days, more services are provided for each—so that higher levels of support are associated with a greater

[21] Frank A. Sloan, "Physician Supply Behavior in the Short Run," *Industrial and Labor Relations Review.* vol. 28 (July 1975), p. 565.
[22] "Financing Health Insurance in Ontario," Budget Paper B, *Ontario Budget 1976*, pp. 6–7.
[23] Ibid., p. 5.
[24] Ibid.
[25] Joseph P. Newhouse, "Towards a Theory of Nonprofit Institutions: An Economic Model of a Hospital," *American Economic Review*, vol. 60 (March 1970), pp. 64–74.

volume of care provided. We assume then that an implicit price for hospital services exists which has a positive relationship to the quantity of services supplied.

The Role of Prices

Fees received for medical services are not determined by the interaction of supply and demand, but rather through negotiation with government officials. In the case of physicians, fees are set by the Ontario Joint Committee on Physicians' Compensation, which reports jointly to the provincial premier and to the president of the Ontario Medical Association. Rather than a unified committee, it consists of three members each from the government and the OMA, and a nonvoting chairman. This committee serves, in effect, as an institutionalized negotiating body.

In a study of the fee-setting process in Ontario, A. Peter Ruderman distinguishes between the structure and the level of fees.[26] He reports that in early negotiations, it was agreed that the structure of fees was "an appropriate responsibility for the profession itself," so that it is determined primarily by the Tariff Committee of the OMA.[27] Moreover, it has been OMA policy to compress fee differentials, and there has been some movement in this direction in recent years.

The level of fees, however, is a different matter. In this area, budgetary considerations play a major role. The increases that political representatives can accept depend on tax and budgetary considerations, and the smaller the increases that are granted, the more funds remain for other programs or for tax cuts. In Ruderman's view, "the parallels between the physicians' fee negotiation and collective bargaining in private industry are rather striking."[28] Here, as elsewhere, there is the implicit threat of a strike that underlies the bargaining process.

Ruderman finds that final outcomes "will depend upon a mixture of political and economic considerations—the ability of the Province to pay an increased amount to physicians without raising taxes or

---

[26] A. Peter Ruderman, "The Economic Position of Ontario Physicians and the Relation between the Schedule of Fees and Actual Income from Fee Practice," in Edward A. Pickering, *Special Study Regarding the Medical Profession in Ontario, A Report to the Ontario Medical Association*, April 1973 (Pickering Report); and A. Peter Ruderman, "The Political Economy of Fee-Setting and the Future of Fee-for-Service," in R.D. Fraser, ed., *Health Economics Symposium, Proceedings of the First Canadian Conference* (Kingston, Ontario: Queens University, 1976), pp. 75–90.

[27] Ruderman, "The Political Economy of Fee-Setting," p. 77.

[28] Ibid., p. 78.

14

premiums, the politicians' appraisal of likely public reaction, and, of course, the nature of the fee proposal put forward by the OMA."[29]

Fees are set in a process of bilateral negotiations in which the relative bargaining strengths of the two sides are critical. On the physician side of the bargaining table, Evans argues that physicians have an implicit target income in mind and a level of fees is sought that would enable them to reach this target. Any decline in actual income below this objective leads directly to "more aggressive fee bargaining, threats of strike, and increased fee schedule settlements."[30] As a result, he expects a *positive* relationship between the number of physicians and the level of fees. An increase in supply leads to lower average workloads, which generate lower incomes and therefore greater pressures to make up the difference through higher fees.

Evans's position requires that physicians seek satisfactory incomes, based largely on existing levels, rather than maximum incomes for given periods of work. There is a presumption here that physicians will be content when an arbitrary income level is reached and, at this point, will refrain from bargaining vigorously for still more.

Whatever the determinants of physicians' bargaining positions, the fees established depend as well on the decisions and actions of the government representatives. While there may be some influence of the quantity of medical services on physicians' negotiating demands, as suggested by Evans, the other factors involved make it unlikely that the relationship between this quantity and the agreed level of fees is either direct or easily determined. Factors outside the medical care system have a major impact on the fee-setting process.

In the case of hospital care, the institutional framework is more complicated since the prices of individual services are not specified explicitly, but, rather, global budgets are set. To be sure, these budgets are influenced by the quantity of services that a hospital expects to provide. Indeed, the budget is based on an expected patient-day load, and a synthetic "per diem" is used for distributing the hospital's budget over the year.[31] Again, reimbursement is determined through negotiations between government representatives and individual hospitals. It remains a bargaining process where government budgetary considerations are crucially important.

---

[29] Ruderman, "The Economic Position of Ontario Physicians," p. 21.
[30] Robert G. Evans, "Does Canada Have Too Many Doctors? Why Nobody Loves an Immigrant Physician," *Canadian Public Policy*, vol. 2 (Spring 1976), p. 150.
[31] Evans, "Beyond the Medical Marketplace," p. 151.

Demand and Supply

The relationship between demand and supply functions for medical services of given quality is given in figure 1.[32] The demand schedule indicated corresponds to Pauly's schedule based on fully accurate information. In the absence of demand generation by physicians, the quantity of services demanded is given where this schedule reaches the horizontal axis, Q_d, since consumers pay a zero monetary price.[33] With demand generation, the actual quantity demanded lies farther to the right. To be sure, this quantity may be very large and therefore lie far to the right in this diagram. After examining the pattern of health care costs and services in Ontario, a recent report concludes in fact that "the demand for health care appears infinite."[34]

The applicable quantity supplied, Q_s, is given by the point on the supply curve at the negotiated price, P_n, for medical services. This figure represents circumstances where there is excess demand for medical services in that Q_d exceeds Q_s. Excess demand, however, may be even greater than the difference between these quantities since, as discussed above, this demand curve is likely to understate the actual quantities demanded. If we are willing to assume that the equilibrium price, P_e, and quantity, Q_e, were reached prior to national health insurance,[35] then there is evidence to support the configuration of demand and supply schedules drawn in figure 1.

Some relevant data are available from a study of physician behavior in Montreal before and after the introduction of government health insurance.[36] Medicare was introduced in Quebec on November 1, 1970, and physician surveys were taken in 1969–1970 and again in 1971–1972. An important finding from these surveys concerns the relationship between the introduction of Medicare and average working hours per physician. "The mean number of hours worked per

---

[32] For an earlier application of demand and supply functions to the market for medical services in Ontario, see R.D. Fraser, *Selected Economic Aspects of the Health Care Sector in Ontario* (Toronto: Province of Ontario, 1970), chap. 5, pp. 68–88.

[33] To be sure, the presence of an effective time price of medical services indicates that the satisfaction point is reached at a smaller level of output, although this is a complication which we ignore.

[34] *Report of the Joint Advisory Committee of the Government of Ontario and the Ontario Medical Association on Methods to Control Health Care Costs* (Toronto: Province of Ontario, December 29, 1977), p. 32.

[35] It is likely, however, that preexisting insurance programs led even then to a greater quantity.

[36] Philip E. Enterline et al., "Effects of 'Free' Medical Care on Medical Practice—The Quebec Experience," *New England Journal of Medicine*, vol. 288 (May 31, 1973), pp. 1152–55; and Philip E. Enterline et al., "Physicians' Working Hours and Patients Seen before and after National Health Insurance," *Medical Care*, vol. 12 (February 1975), pp. 95–103.

day was 10.3 prior to Medicare and 8.8 after,"[37] which is a decline of nearly 15 percent. Moreover, "the proportion of physicians working 12 hours or more dropped from 37 percent prior to Medicare to 17 percent after, while the proportion of physicians working less than eight hours increased from 18 percent before Medicare to 28 percent after."[38]

Not only did the quantity of labor supplied decline, but also the composition of physician services changed substantially. The number of patient contracts per weekday by Montreal physicians fell from 82,262 before the introduction of government health insurance to 74,463 after, or by nearly 9.5 percent.[39] This decline, however, consisted of two types of patient contact: telephone consultations fell by 10,538 per day, or by 41 percent; and home visits fell from 2,914 per day to 1,080, a decline of 63 percent. On the other hand, there was an increase in office visits from 23,840 to 31,509 per day, or 32 percent. The average time spent with each patient in these visits, however, fell by 16 percent.[40]

With the introduction of national health insurance, there was an apparent change in the structure of incentives faced by physicians. There occurred a shift in the relative gains from providing different services, favoring office visits at the expense of other types of patient contact. To permit the sharp increase in the number of office visits that occurred, the number of telephone consultations and home visits declined, as did the average time spent per office visit.

These new incentives led physicians to provide more services and submit more claims than they did before. Not only was there a propensity to provide more services to regular patients but also to bill for services previously provided without charge. The latter include those rendered on a charitable basis or as professional courtesy, or because there was a substantial clinical research component.[41]

On both accounts, there was an increase in the measured quantity of physician services supplied. This change took place despite a decline in the average number of hours worked. If we were willing to ignore any change in the quality of services provided,[42] these results would necessarily indicate a shift to the right in the supply schedule

---

[37] Enterline, "Physicians' Working Hours," p. 98.
[38] Ibid.
[39] Enterline, "Effects of 'Free' Medical Care," p. 1154.
[40] Ibid.
[41] M.G. Brown, A. Benham, and L. Benham, "The Introduction of Medicare in Canada and Windfall Gains to Physicians," unpublished paper, October 1976, p. 11.
[42] For a discussion of the relationship between a physician's patient load per hour and the quality of his services, see Uwe E. Reinhardt, *Physician Productivity and the Demand for Health Manpower* (Cambridge, Mass.: Ballinger, 1975), pp. 251–58.

of physician services. As long as the demand schedule and average fees received per claim remain unchanged, this shift implies that the quantity of services supplied exceeds the new equilibrium quantity.

An increase in average fees would lead to a still greater difference between these quantities. Although posted fee schedules were generally unchanged, there is some indication that actual fees received may have increased. Prior to national health insurance, fees actually billed were often lower than posted schedules. Moreover, uncollected fees often exceeded the 10 and 15 percent figures incorporated in the Medicare payment formulas so that the effective level of fees increased.[43]

That this type of change took place with the imposition of national health insurance is supported by the common observation that "the single most prominent influence of health insurance in Canada has been to increase the earnings of health providers."[44] Thus, between 1969 and 1971 physician net earnings in Quebec increased by 51.0 percent, while average wages and salaries rose by 15.6 percent, indicating a relative income gain exceeding 30 percent. The corresponding figures for Ontario are less pronounced: during the first full year under Medicare, physician net earnings increased by 21.5 percent, compared with an increase in weekly wages and salaries of 15.9 percent. The relative income gain of physicians therefore was 4.8 percent.[45]

Furthermore, prior to Medicare, patients in Quebec waited an average of six days to obtain an appointment with their physicians. Following the introduction of government health insurance, this period jumped to eleven days, an increase of over 80 percent.[46] If this finding were applied to Ontario, it would also suggest that the quantities of medical services demanded exceeded the quantities supplied.

The Gains and Losses from Supply Restrictions

As indicated above, the optimal quantity of medical services is given by the equilibrium value, Q_e. When a larger quantity is provided and consumed, consumers are receiving care on which they place a lower value than the corresponding opportunity cost. While consumers'

---

[43] Brown, Benham, and Benham, "The Introduction of Medicare in Canada."
[44] Evans, "Beyond the Medical Marketplace," p. 133.
[45] Ibid., p. 134. Further evidence regarding this gain throughout Canada is reported in Brown, Benham, and Benham, "The Introduction of Medicare in Canada," pp. 3–10.
[46] Enterline, "The Distribution of Medical Services," p. 1176.

valuation is positive, it is still less than the effective additional cost of the services to society in terms of the alternatives forgone. Thus, there is a welfare loss from an excess quantity of services provided.

The effect of limiting the maximum number of physicians who may practice in Ontario is to define a new supply function for medical services, drawn as S' in figure 1. This schedule is vertical, since the restraint is imposed without reference to price. If there is excess demand for services, then this limitation on the number of physicians and hospital beds will lead to fewer services provided, represented by a decline from Q_s to Q_p. Moreover, even in the absence of excess demand for these services, a decline in the number of physicians might well reduce the volume of services generated by physicians, with similar results. Where neither mechanism is present, a policy of restricting the supply of physicians would be largely ineffective. Such would be the case if Q_d lay between Q_e and Q_p.

Given the configuration in figure 1, the gains from this policy action are readily indicated. Government outlays on health care services are reduced by the rectangular area which is the aggregate of areas $1 + 2 + 3$. This sum is the reduction in quantity, $Q_s - Q_p$, times the negotiated price, P_a.

A part of this savings represents a loss to physicians who would otherwise wish to practice in Ontario. All is not lost, however, since presumably those physicians who are prevented from practicing in Ontario will ply their trade elsewhere. Yet their wish to practice in Ontario suggests a willingness to pay something more for the privilege than they would for their next preferred opportunity. The opportunity cost of practicing elsewhere is reflected in the supply price of their services and should be deducted from earnings received in Ontario. The producer surplus that remains is indicated by area 1 in figure 1. This amount represents a cost to providers of a policy of restricting supply.

In addition, the value imputed by consumers to the medical services forgone represents a further cost of this policy. This consumer surplus is measured conventionally by the area under a compensated demand curve and is here indicated by area 3. Although government expenditures are reduced, there is a corresponding loss to those consumers who would wish to consume more medical services than they will now be able to do. This loss, however, is smaller than the savings which accrue to the taxpayers of the province.

The quantity remaining is area 2, which is the difference between the savings to the taxpayers of Ontario and the opportunity costs of this policy to both consumers and producers. This area represents the welfare gains resulting from the imposition of supply restraints

FIGURE 2

GAINS AND LOSSES FROM SUPPLY RESTRICTIONS

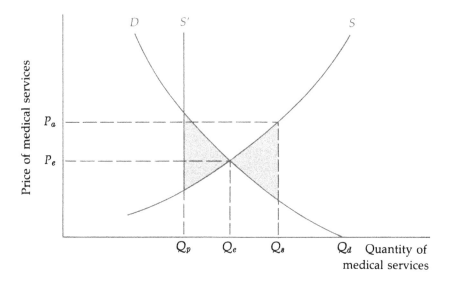

and indicates the net loss to society of permitting the quantity of medical services to increase from Q_p to Q_s. Depending on the relevant elasticities of demand and supply, the welfare gains from this policy action may be quite large, and the total savings to taxpayers even larger.

As can be seen, the gains from restricting supply to the optimal quantity Q_e would be still larger. The net gain would then be given by the shaded triangle to the right of Q_e in figure 2. Note that this optimum could also be reached if the price for services was dropped to P_e. Moreover, government outlays would be reduced by the difference in price times the optimal quantity. These savings would accrue to taxpayers at the expense of the providers of medical services even though the quantity of services would remain the same.

Although the optimal number of physicians in Ontario would be reached, the decision to set lower fee schedules would influence the particular physicians who choose to practice in Ontario. Practitioners who have fairly high opportunity costs of their services, because of the ability to practice in, say, the United States, might well depart from Ontario for more lucrative pastures. Those physicians, on the other hand, who have fairly low opportunity costs, because income levels in their home countries are quite low, would come to Ontario to practice. Thus, there is some support for the view that the setting of lower prices for health care services would lead to a substantial restructuring of the medical profession. At the same time, it should be clear that the public bears a substantial cost for maintaining the current structure and organization of the profession.

While there may be significant gains to be had from restricting the supply of physicians in circumstances where the quantity of medical services exceeds the optimum, there may also be substantial losses associated with overshooting the mark and restricting supply too much. A diagrammatic representation of this problem is also given in figure 2. While the gains from restricting the supply of physicians from Q_s to Q_e are indicated by the shaded area to the right of Q_e, the welfare loss from excessive supply restrictions—from the movement, say, from Q_e to Q_p—is given by the shaded area to the left of Q_e. This area represents the extent to which the sum of consumer surplus and producer surplus forgone by the successive restrictions on supply exceeds the tax revenues that are saved. Where the net losses and gains are approximately equal, as suggested in the diagram, there will be no welfare gain from moving to Q_p, compared with staying at the original point, Q_s.

A major difficulty with physical allocation policies such as the one adopted in Ontario is determining how much restraint is enough and how much is too much. The magnitudes of the relevant parameters are difficult to measure, and yet it is on the basis of these parameters that specific judgments on physical allocation must be made. For the most part, policy makers in Ontario have relied on World Health Organization standards to set rough benchmarks for their actions.

In the absence of fees paid by consumers, the quantity of medical services in Ontario is essentially a political decision. Decision makers cannot rely on the actions of individual consumers as reflected in market transactions, since essentially the market has been abolished, except to the extent that an implicit time price is paid by waiting in line. Government decisions concerning the appropriate levels of costs and services are all that remain. The need to rely on arbitrary standards is a characteristic feature of policy actions of this type.

3

Measuring the Effects of Supply Limitations

The previous chapter indicated that society may realize substantial gains by placing physical limits on the supply of medical services. This conclusion rests on the configuration of supply and demand schedules drawn in figure 1. Although fragmentary evidence supporting this configuration is provided, there is no overall empirical analysis of the underlying relationships.

This chapter provides empirical evidence bearing on these relationships. Although supply and demand functions are not estimated directly, the effects of various aspects of both on the quantity of medical services are investigated. Both physician services and bed-days of care in Ontario hospitals are included.

The purpose of this chapter is to estimate the prospective effect of government actions to limit both the number of physicians and the stock of available hospital beds on the volume of medical services. As long as these actions restrict increases in both physicians and beds, population growth would lead to fewer numbers per capita. Throughout, it is assumed that there are no other changes in government policies toward health care.

A Framework of Analysis

There are three alternative explanations why the number of physicians should affect the volume of services consumed. First, these markets may be characterized by excess demand. That is, at the zero monetary price faced by most consumers, the public may demand more services than physicians wish to supply at the price negotiated with government representatives. This configuration of supply and demand schedules is indicated in figure 1. In such circumstances, any decline in the number of physicians will reduce the quantity of services consumed because supply is the controlling factor.

Second, even if there is no excess demand for their services, physicians may influence consumption by the type of information they provide jointly with their services. Since there are alternative forms of therapy and substantial variability in their efficacy among patients, it may be possible to recommend different treatment to patients presenting similar symptoms. Moreover, physicians might be expected to encourage the consumption of more services if they are less busy, but of fewer services if they are more busy. Thus, a larger number of physicians, each initially less busy, might result in advice leading to a greater demand for medical care.[1]

Third, the number of available physicians may influence the time cost to patients in terms of transportation, waiting, and inconvenience in obtaining physicians' services. Travel distances on the average should be shorter and waiting times lessened were there more physicians. Thus, even without excess demand, a larger number of physicians may result in reduced time costs, leading directly to an increased demand for services.[2]

Any one of these factors would lead to a positive relationship between the number of physicians and the volume of services. From this analysis, there is no way of distinguishing the effects of the different factors. To be sure, a positive relationship is also consistent with an original position in which the quantity supplied equals the quantity demanded at Q_e in figure 1. This finding, therefore, cannot demonstrate that the quantity of medical services exceeds the social optimum. That conclusion must rest on the factors discussed in chapter 2. A positive finding would indicate the strength of the relationship between the relevant supply factors and the quantity of medical services—whether direct and/or indirect through demand creation and time prices—as well as the prospective effectiveness of policy measures to restrain supply.

---

[1] For some discussion of this effect in Canada, see Robert G. Evans, "Supplier-Induced Demand: Some Empirical Evidence and Implications," in Mark Perlman, ed., *The Economics of Health and Medical Care* (New York: Wiley, 1974), pp. 162–73. See also the discussion in chapter 2 above.

[2] A recent study of the demand for medical care in the United States reports that "travel time (as measured by distance) functions as a price in determining the demand for medical services when free care is available." Jon Paul Acton, "Nonmonetary Factors in the Demand for Medical Services: Some Empirical Evidence," *Journal of Political Economy*, vol. 83 (June 1975), p. 610.

In the absence of an observed relationship, one would conclude that there was no net effect of these factors at the margin. Consistent with that finding would be the result that the quantity of medical services supplied at the negotiated price exceeds the quantity demanded at a zero monetary price—that excess supply is present rather than excess demand. In this case, measures to limit the supply of physicians and hospital beds would not generally lead to a reduced volume of services.

In markets for medical services, not only is the quantity of services demanded likely to depend on the available supply, but this demand may also depend, at least in part, on the medical requirements of the patients as perceived by physicians. In the practice of medicine, the quantity of services provided may depend on the pathology observed as well as on the choice between income and leisure that otherwise determines the volume of services physicians wish to provide. Even where excess demand exists, therefore, demand conditions can be expected to influence the quantity of services supplied.

For these reasons, elements of both supply and demand should determine the quantity of medical services. We estimate this relationship in the analysis below. Various regression equations are specified in which the dependent variables represent the quantities of physician services and hospital services.

Our primary concern is with those elements of the supply function that are subject to policy actions: the number of physicians and the quantity of hospital beds per capita. The hypothesis examined is that these factors have a positive effect on the quantity of services provided, since this hypothesis is implicit in recent government decisions. In the equations explaining physician services, only the number of physicians is included, while the supply both of physicians and of hospital beds are included in the equations dealing with hospital services. Medical fees, however, are not included since there is little observed variability.

To be sure, the number of physicians depends on factors besides government policy. In particular, the quantity of physicians in an area may depend on the demand for their services, especially if income levels can be influenced. It is necessary, therefore, to incorporate any reverse effect of the volume of services on the number of physicians in the estimating procedures.

We also include a further element of supply in these equations: the number of registered nurses in the physician services equations, and the number of hospital nurses in the hospital services equations. These variables are intended to test whether a greater quantity of nurses increases physician and hospital productivity so that a larger volume of services is provided for a given number of physicians and hospital beds. In such circumstances, the supply of nurses would have a positive effect on the quantity of medical services provided.

Variables reflecting the demand for services are also required. These should include illness rates among specific groups in the population, as well as other factors that increase the proclivity of patients to seek medical assistance. These factors, however, are difficult to define and have little direct connection with the policy issues mentioned above.

In the regression equations, arbitrary demographic and economic characteristics of the population are included as explanatory variables. These variables are designed not so much to test specific hypotheses as to account for the impact of demand conditions generally. They are included in the equations primarily so that the remaining coefficients will not encompass the influence of extraneous factors.

Empirical Results for Physician Services

For this analysis, data were gathered on an annual basis for each of eight payment districts in Ontario for each of three years. In the middle of this period, Mississauga was created as a separate district, largely out of Toronto.[3] Data for Mississauga, however, did not appear comparable with that of the other districts and therefore were excluded from the analysis. We assume here that the underlying observations are fully independent. Yet, there is some prospect that this assumption is violated, owing to the export of services from one district to another.

If patients residing in a district could not move across district boundaries in search of medical care, no problem would arise. To the extent, however, that a patient living in one area goes to another in search of medical care, statistics on the quantity of services provided refer to the district to which he went rather than to the district from which he came. Much border-crossing of this type might signify that the quantity of physician services provided in a district may be positively related to the supply of physicians, but not for the reasons suggested above. More services are provided in districts where there are more physicians per capita, but only so long as there is excess demand for services in districts where these patients in fact reside. If there were no excess demand for specific services at home, individuals presumably would not go to the trouble of traveling in search

---

[3] Because of a change in reporting, the Toronto district has different boundaries in some years than in others. Observations for each year, however, are defined on a comparable basis.

of care. Thus, a positive relationship may result from an imbalance of supply and demand in different districts, even in the absence of excess demand or of demand creation throughout Ontario.

Movement across districts in search of care by specialists could be substantial. In that case, the estimated equations may not measure the effect of the number of specialists overall on the total volume of services provided. At least part of the estimated effect will reflect the movement of patients. While evidence on this matter is sparse, we would expect to find some patient search for specialists, and therefore the estimated coefficients will be biased upwards. Government actions to limit the supply of specialists may therefore have less restraining influence on the volume of services provided than is suggested in the regression equations. The empirical estimates therefore represent an upper bound on the likely effects of a program of supply restraint.

The dependent variable in these equations is the number of medical claims per capita paid by the Ontario Health Insurance Plan, multiplied by the average cost per claim in the relevant district and year.[4] Medical claims represent the unit of account of OHIP payments, and, on average, indicate 1.83 services. A service denotes what a physician is paid for, which might be an office visit, a laboratory procedure, a consultation, or even an operation. Since the number of services per claim varies, it is particularly important to adjust each observation according to average costs per claim. Thus, districts which provide, on average, more services per claim, or a higher value of these services as reflected in the OHIP payment schedule, are represented as providing more physician services.

A difficulty with this measure of physician services is that it depends on the structure of fees.[5] As indicated above, this structure is set largely by the Ontario Medical Association and does not necessarily reflect consumer marginal valuations. The services of higher-paid physicians will therefore indicate greater output than those of their lower-paid counterparts, even though consumers may be indifferent between the two. To the extent that specialists are paid more to provide the same services than are general practitioners, total output is greater where there are more specialists. This measure of services provided, therefore, reflects not only actual output, but also the relative importance of higher-priced inputs.

---

[4] This variable is not defined simply as costs per capita since the average cost per claim differs in each of the three years.

[5] No adjustments for changes in the composition of physician fee schedules were made. While such adjustments would have led to a more accurate measure of services provided, data to make such adjustments were unavailable.

The major explanatory variable is the number of active physicians per capita in a given district and year. Physicians are divided between general practitioners and specialists on the basis of reports by the College of Physicians and Surgeons. Although it was possible to obtain information on the distribution of specific specialty types, these data were not used because the ratios of the various specialty types to population were highly collinear across districts.[6] Moreover, while the different specialties may have different effects on the volume of both physician and hospital services, policy discussions have generally focused on the number of specialists overall. That discussion, as well as this analysis, is based on the premise that, whatever other actions are taken, the distribution of specialty types will remain generally unchanged.

The other variables included in the analysis are the number of registered nurses in the district, average family income, and the proportions of the population that live in urban areas and that are children, female, and over sixty-five years old. In addition, population density, the presence or absence of a medical school in the district, and district population are used as instruments in the two-stage least squares equations. Data on family income and the various population characteristics are obtained from the 1971 *Census of Canada* and thus are available only for that year. As a result, there are only eight observations for these particular explanatory variables, and we are wary of placing much reliance on their regression coefficients. Even where observations for each year are available, the residuals over time are likely to be correlated, and therefore the statistical tests applied should be interpreted with caution. The data sources for all of the variables are reported in the appendix.

The regression equations are presented in table 1.[7] Separate intercepts are estimated for each year to reflect differences in the use of physician services across the three years. The equations are estimated both by ordinary least squares and by two-stage least squares. The latter procedure accounts for the fact that the numbers of general practitioners (GPs) and of specialists per capita are appropriately considered endogenous, since these values are influenced by the demand for services in the particular district. Since we cannot specify all of the prospective determinants of the supply of physicians, however,

---

[6] This effect of collinearity showed itself by the presence of high standard errors of regression coefficients in some similar equations.

[7] The significance of the estimated coefficients for the various supply factors is determined on the basis of a one-tail test in which the null hypothesis is that the supply of, say, physicians does not have a positive effect on the quantity of services provided. In the case of family income and the various demographic factors, where there is no hypothesized sign, a two-tail test is used.

TABLE 1

REGRESSION EQUATIONS EXPLAINING PHYSICIAN SERVICES PROVIDED PER CAPITA

Estimation Method	Intercepts			No. of GPs per Capita	No. of Specialists per Capita	No. of RNs per Capita	Average Family Income	Proportion of Population			
	1972–73	1973–74	1974–75					In urban areas	Children	Female	Over 65
1. OLSQ	– 2.89 (0.18)	– 2.20 (0.14)	– 1.86 (0.12)	– 2.93 (3.36)	7.28** (4.47)	—	– 0.000138 (0.78)	3.78** (3.80)	15.62* (2.51)	– 8.77 (0.27)	14.48 (1.09)
2. 2SLSQ	–36.49 (1.08)	–35.83 (1.06)	35.73 (1.05)	– 1.08 (0.54)	6.50* (2.29)	—	– 0.000123 (0.43)	3.60* (2.26)	28.55* (2.28)	–48.81 (0.76)	– 0.42 (0.02)
3. OLSQ	–16.92 (1.00)	–16.26 (0.96)	–16.13 (0.94)	– 2.95 (3.58)	6.98** (4.55)	0.379* (1.72)	– 0.000059 (0.35)	5.02** (4.27)	24.82** (3.15)	6.09 (0.19)	6.46 (0.49)
4. 2SLSQ	–36.36 (1.08)	–35.70 (1.06)	–36.61 (1.05)	– 1.19 (0.53)	6.55* (2.32)	0.040 (0.09)	– 0.000116 (0.39)	3.74 (1.65)	29.02* (2.11)	47.53 (0.73)	– 0.65 (0.03)

NOTE: Equations estimated from 24 observations; figures in parentheses are t values.

**Statistically significant at the 1% confidence level.
*Statistically significant at the 5% confidence level.

the former estimates are also of interest. The dependent variable is measured by medical claims per person, while both GPs and specialists per capita are measured by the number of physicians per thousand of the population.

As can be seen, the results depend on which estimation method is used, in one important respect. While the number of specialists per capita has a *positive* and significant coefficient in all cases, the coefficient of the number of GPs per capita is *negative* throughout. When the reverse effect of the volume of services on the number of general practitioners is taken into account, however, the estimated coefficient is only about half its standard error and cannot be distinguished statistically from zero.

What these findings indicate is that, holding the number of general practitioners constant, a reduction in the supply of specialists leads to a substantial decline in the volume of services. On the other hand, holding the number of specialists constant, there is no indication that a decline in GPs per capita would lead to the provision of fewer services.

This conclusion, however, depends on our index of medical services—the quantity of individual services multiplied by their corresponding fees. Since fees of specialists are generally higher than those of GPs per unit of time spent in providing care, the observed results are influenced by this factor. At the same time, the quantity of physician services measured in this manner is likely to be more closely related to the aggregate cost of medical services than are unweighted measures; and costs serve as an essential focus of this study.

Different market circumstances apparently apply to the two groups of physicians. In the case of specialists, there may be excess demand for their services. Alternatively, specialist physicians may be particularly able to influence the volume of services that they provide to each patient. While it may be difficult to determine this quantity totally—so as to reach fully a desired income level—specialists may have sufficient control over what is done that more of them per capita will lead each to "suggest" more care and provide more services.

For general practitioners, on the other hand, the quantity of services provided to each patient may be far less malleable. A critical decision in this regard is whether or not to recommend that a patient consult a specialist. Furthermore, there is no indication that excess demand exists for these services—at the prices paid by patients and received by these physicians. A small decline in the supply of these physicians may thus have little or no effect on the volume of services provided.

Some further information can be drawn from the size of the

estimated coefficients. At the mean values of the dependent and independent variables, and using the coefficients reported in equation 4, the elasticity of physician services with respect to the number of GPs is −0.22, which, however, is not statistically different from zero. The elasticity with respect to specialists, on the other hand, is +0.93.[8]

Another implication of these findings concerns the effect of changing the number of physicians per capita without changing the ratio of general practitioners to specialists. Given the relative sizes of the estimated coefficients, we obtain the expected result that a reduced supply of physicians tends to reduce the volume of services provided. Combining the two estimated elasticities, the overall elasticity of physician services with respect to the number of physicians is +0.71. A 10 percent decline in the number of physicians is thereby associated with a 7 percent decline in the volume of services, as long as the ratio of GPs to specialists is unchanged. With a decline in the number of physicians, therefore, those who remain can be expected to increase their output of services, so that the overall quantity of services will decline, but not by as much as the decline in the total number of physicians.

A further result concerns the effect of the number of registered nurses in Ontario. Although the relevant coefficient is positive and significant when the equation is estimated by ordinary least squares, it approaches zero when multi-equation methods are used. This variable appears to have no independent effect on the volume of *physician* services provided. What this finding indicates is that increasing the number of nurses per physician is not likely to expand the volume of medical services. There is no suggestion that physicians provide more services when assisted by a larger number of nurses.

Of the remaining variables in this equation, only the proportions of the population consisting of children and living in urban areas have significant coefficients, suggesting that these factors lead to an increased volume of services consumed. It is noteworthy that there is no significant effect of family income on the quantity of services

---

[8] This final coefficient is somewhat larger than expected. If there is no change in the volume of services provided per specialist, and if the ratio of services supplied by GPs to those supplied by specialists is 47:53, then a 1 percent decline in the number of specialists, holding the number of GPs constant, would lead to a reduction in the volume of all physician services provided of 0.53 percent—rather than the estimated 0.93 percent. The ratio 47:53 rests on two factors: first, in 1974 GPs accounted for 56 percent of all physicians in Ontario. In addition, for the payment year 1975–1976, the average cost per service (as contrasted to claim) was $5.94 for GPs and $8.43 for specialists. No account is taken of any differences in the average number of services provided between the two types of physicians. Ministry of Health, Province of Ontario, *Statistical Report on OHIP Medical Experience, 1974–1975* (Toronto, June 1975), table 13, p. 45.

received. Although a positive coefficient for the proportion of the population over sixty-five years old was anticipated, the observed two-stage least squares estimates, which are effectively zero, may have resulted from collinearity with other exploratory variables. Again, these variables are not of primary interest and are intended merely to represent general demand conditions.

Empirical Results for Hospital Care

In the analysis of hospital care, the dependent variables are the number of bed-days per capita of a particular type of care provided in public active and in chronic hospitals. The number of bed-days of hospital care in each category is weighted by the ratio of approved net allowable ward costs per diem[9] in the district to the appropriate average value throughout the province in the particular year. While the same weighting scheme is used for all types of care, it does provide some means of adjusting for the prospect that output may not be homogeneous across hospitals.[10] We again assume that more medical services are provided in hospitals where costs per diem are higher.

Note also that data on hospital care were available on a calendar rather than a fiscal-year basis, as were the data for physician services. As a result, the two parts of the empirical analysis in this study are not easily combined.

Similar regression equations are estimated. There are two new explanatory variables: nurses per capita, which here is limited to full-time hospital registered nurses, and hospital capacity in terms of the number of beds available and staffed. In these equations, we include the supply of both types of physicians, of available beds, and of nurses as separate factors determining the weighted number of bed-days of care provided. The empirical results that deal with acute hospital care are given in table 2.

In equations 1 and 2, all of the explanatory variables are included together. The supply of beds has a positive coefficient in each case, although the coefficients are not statistically significant at conventional levels. On the other hand, the number of hospital nurses has a far lower coefficient and quite low t values. In the case of physicians,

---

[9] Net allowable ward costs are the difference between gross operating costs and offset revenues. The latter largely comprise: 1) revenues from private and semi-private accommodations, and 2) out-patient receipts. These costs thereby represent the cost of providing services on a standard ward basis.

[10] See Seymour Berki, *Hospital Economics* (Lexington, Mass.: Heath, 1972), p. 37.

TABLE 2

REGRESSION EQUATIONS EXPLAINING THE NUMBER OF WEIGHTED BED-DAYS OF ACUTE CARE AT PUBLIC GENERAL HOSPITALS PER CAPITA

Estimation Method	Intercepts			No. of GPs per Capita	No. of Specialists per Capita	No. of Full-time Hospital RNs per Capita	No. of Acute Beds Staffed per Capita	Average Family Income	Proportion of Population			
	1972	1973	1974						In urban areas	Children	Female	Over 65
1. OLSQ	3.16 (0.49)	3.08 (0.48)	3.08 (0.48)	0.377 (1.20)	1.244* (2.09)	0.00095 (0.01)	0.0974 (1.51)	-0.0000927* (2.36)	0.0334 (0.15)	3.37* (2.86)	-7.37 (0.57)	1.00 (0.20)
2. 2SLSQ	-1.69 (0.20)	-1.75 (0.21)	-1.78 (0.21)	0.897* (1.86)	0.519 (0.61)	0.0671 (0.69)	0.117 (1.48)	-0.0000923* (2.04)	-0.0704 (0.27)	2.63* (1.88)	3.02 (0.18)	-3.53 (0.54)
3. OLSQ	11.20* (2.97)	11.10* (2.95)	11.08* (2.93)	0.127 (0.46)	1.904** (4.52)	0.0642 (0.89)	—	-0.000129** (3.98)	-0.122 (0.57)	2.76* (2.38)	-22.48* (2.57)	3.655 (0.74)
4. 2SLSQ	7.35 (1.52)	7.26 (1.50)	7.21 (1.48)	0.667 (1.54)	1.204* (1.92)	0.1566 (1.61)	—	-0.000138** (3.67)	-0.283 (1.08)	1.70 (1.15)	-13.64 (1.21)	-1.09 (0.17)
5. OLSQ	13.97** (6.78)	13.86** (6.73)	13.85** (6.72)	-0.051 (0.27)	2.184** (8.10)	—	—	-0.000113** (5.48)	—	3.40** (3.92)	-29.11** (6.61)	7.69** (3.94)
6. 2SLSQ	14.10** (6.39)	14.00** (6.34)	13.98** (6.34)	0.186 (0.80)	1.944** (5.77)	—	—	-0.0000996** (4.30)	—	3.31** (3.08)	-29.82** (6.13)	8.58** (4.04)

NOTE: Equations estimated from 24 observations; figures in parentheses are t values.

**Statistically significant at the 1% confidence level.
*Statistically significant at the 5% confidence level.

the results are mixed. Where the equation is estimated by ordinary least squares, the number of general practitioners is positive but not statistically significant, while the number of specialists is larger and statistically significant. Where the equation is estimated by two-stage least squares, to account for any reverse causality, the relative size of the two coefficients is reversed, and now the number of general practitioners is statistically significant.

In equations 3 and 4, the number of acute beds is removed from the equation. When this is done, the number of specialists per capita remains positive and significant with both estimation methods, while the coefficient for the number of general practitioners is now smaller and not significant. An implication of these findings is that the number of specialists is related to the supply of beds in their effect on the volume of hospital services provided, so it is difficult to distinguish the separate effects of each. This implication seems especially likely since a large number of specialists are hospital-based, practicing largely or entirely within hospitals. As a result, supply conditions for hospital beds and for specialists may be closely tied.

This result is also indicated in equations 5 and 6, in which two more variables are dropped. In addition to the number of hospital nurses employed, the proportion of the population located in urban areas is eliminated, as this variable is closely correlated with average family income. The estimated coefficients for the number of specialists per capita are larger than before and highly significant. Moreover, the number of general practitioners is far less important and approaches zero. What is suggested by these findings is that the number of specialists in an area and the number of available beds are the primary factors which determine the volume of acute hospital services in Ontario.

As before, we can compute the responsiveness of weighted bed-days of hospital care to changes in various explanatory variables. At the mean values for each of these variables, and using the estimates given in equation 1, the elasticity with respect to GPs is 0.19 and with respect to specialists is 0.50, while the elasticity with respect to beds staffed is 0.34. In the case of specialists per capita, this elasticity falls to 0.21 when it is based on the coefficient estimated in equation 2, but jumps to 0.89 in equation 5 and to 0.79 in equation 6. Note that the sum of the elasticities for specialists and for beds staffed from equation 1 is 0.84, which is midway between the two elasticities for specialists alone from equations 5 and 6.

We also examine the influence of various demographic features of the population. The estimated coefficient for average family income is negative and statistically significant in all equations. Thus, it appears that less wealthy families have a need or a preference for more in-hospital care. Furthermore, there is some indication that the proportion of the population made up of children has a positive impact on the volume of hospital care provided. Moreover, the number of full-time hospital nurses employed has a positive coefficient when it is included in the equations, but the coefficients are never statistically significant.

We also investigate the determinants of the volume of chronic care provided at both public general and chronic hospitals. The estimated equations are given in table 3. In equations 1 and 2, all variables are included except the number of hospital nurses, since available data do not refer to chronic cases alone. As reported, the number of general practitioners has a negative coefficient throughout. In contrast, the number of specialists per capita has a positive and significant coefficient. A negative coefficient in these equations would suggest that, holding the number of specialists constant, an increased supply of general practitioners leads to less chronic care provided in hospitals.

This finding indicates that the services of general practitioners are, to some extent, substitutable with this type of in-patient care. On the other hand, holding the number of GPs constant, an increased number of specialists per capita leads to a greater volume of hospital services for chronic patients. The number of specialists appears therefore to be complementary with hospital services. Also consistent with these findings is the likelihood that services by general practitioners to chronic patients are provided largely on an out-patient basis, while those of specialists are more frequently provided within the confines of a hospital. A surprising implication of these equations is that the number of staffed chronic beds appears to have little effect on the volume of chronic care provided.

Again, we compute the associated elasticities at mean values. Based on the coefficients given in equation 1, the elasticity for the number of general practitioners is -0.47 while the elasticity for the number of specialists is $+1.87$. These findings indicate that there may be substantial differences between GPs and specialists in their provision of hospital care for chronic patients and that the relative effects may be quite large. Moreover, if the number of physicians is increased while the ratio of GPs to specialists is held constant, the resulting elasticity is $+1.40$. That is, a 1 percent increase in the number of both general practitioners and specialists increases the quantity of hospital services used by chronic patients by 1.4 percent.

From the results presented in table 3, we also observe that the coefficients for average family income are always negative and sta-

TABLE 3

REGRESSION EQUATIONS EXPLAINING THE NUMBER OF WEIGHTED BED-DAYS OF CHRONIC CARE AT PUBLIC GENERAL AND CHRONIC HOSPITALS PER CAPITA

(includes care in special rehabilitation and general rehabilitation units)

Estimation Method	Intercepts			No. of GPs per Capita	No. of Specialists per Capita	No. of Chronic Beds Staffed per Capita	Average Family Income	Proportion of Population			
	1972	1973	1974					In urban areas	Children	Female	Over 65
1. OLSQ	5.07* (2.32)	5.05* (2.31)	5.05* (2.31)	−0.208 (1.48)	1.307** (4.20)	−0.039 (0.55)	−0.0000527* (2.23)	−0.100 (0.90)	−1.037 (1.29)	−8.445* (2.06)	1.168 (0.78)
2. 2SLSQ	4.96* (2.23)	4.95* (2.22)	4.95* (2.22)	−0.269 (1.65)	1.092** (4.05)	−0.036 (0.49)	−0.0000550* (2.25)	−0.106 (0.95)	−1.001 (1.22)	−8.148* (1.95)	0.909 (0.59)
3. OLSQ	4.19* (2.89)	4.17* (2.88)	4.17* (2.88)	−0.184 (1.41)	0.953** (5.06)	—	−0.0000449* (2.43)	−0.111 (1.04)	−0.756 (1.24)	−7.023* (2.27)	0.891 (0.65)
4. 2SLSQ	4.15* (2.85)	4.13* (2.84)	4.13* (2.84)	−0.223 (1.47)	0.984** (4.74)	—	−0.0000467* (2.48)	−0.116 (1.08)	−0.779 (1.26)	−6.837* (2.19)	0.740 (0.53)

NOTE: Equations estimated from 24 observations; figures in parentheses are t values.

**Statistically significant at 1% confidence level.
*Statistically significant at 5% confidence level.

tistically significant. Higher incomes appear to have a depressing effect on the quantity of chronic care sought and received, although the finding may also be due to the reverse effect whereby being chronically ill may lead to substantially lower incomes. As a result, we cannot draw any conclusions as to the importance of this factor.

In equations 3 and 4, the number of staffed chronic beds is omitted from the equations, but the results are generally comparable to those discussed above. These findings therefore provide some confirmation of the negative effect of general practitioners on the volume of chronic hospital care.

Conclusions

Our primary empirical finding concerns the separate effects of the supplies of GPs and of specialists on the provision of medical care. For the most part, the number of general practitioners plays a minor role in determining the overall quantity of medical services. Specialists, on the other hand, have a major influence on the provision of these services, although in the case of both acute and chronic hospital care, it is difficult to distinguish the effect of their presence from that of bed availability. The apparent differences between general practitioners and specialists represent the most striking conclusion to be drawn from this analysis.

These findings can be compared with those published by Victor Fuchs and Marcia Kramer for the United States.[11] In the first equation in their model, they examine the impact of the number of physicians per capita on the quantity of physician services provided per capita in a particular state. Their measure of the quantity of services provided reflects largely the number of visits to physicians. Other explanatory variables include prices, average patient incomes, and the importance of medical insurance. Since the economic incentives facing patients are different between the two countries, our concern here is primarily with reported findings on the effect of the number of physicians per capita.

In every specification of this equation, they report a positive and significant impact of the number of physicians on the quantity of services provided. The relevant elasticities lie between $+0.3$ and $+0.5$.[12] Although no division is made between general practitioners

---

[11] Victor R. Fuchs and Marcia J. Kramer, *Determinants of Expenditures for Physicians' Services in the United States, 1948–1968* (Washington, D.C.: National Center for Health Services Research and Development, Department of Health, Education, and Welfare, December 1972).

[12] Ibid., p. 31.

and specialists, as is done here, their findings for the United States are not too different from the overall elasticity reported above of +0.71. Despite the different medical care systems in the two countries, similar behavioral relationships seem to apply.

4

Lessons from the Ontario Experience

In previous chapters, we investigated the empirical and conceptual implications of a policy designed to restrict the quantities of physicians and of hospital beds in Ontario. We found that, under the current medical care system in Ontario, there is some support for a program of supply restraint as applied to medical specialists.

In this chapter, we focus directly on the pattern of policy making in Ontario. We examine the policies adopted, their relationship to earlier policies, and their advantages and disadvantages. This pattern of policy actions and reactions provides a useful guide to what may occur if similar actions were taken in the United States. Our primary object is to uncover what significance the Ontario experience may have for public policy in the United States.

A Pattern for Policy Making

Since the adoption of national health insurance, expenditures on medical care in Ontario have jumped sharply. During the five-year period between 1970–1971 and 1975–1976, spending on insured services increased from $1.2 billion to nearly $2.5 billion, or by over 100 percent.[1] While this was partly due to the general rate of inflation,

---

[1] "Financing Health Insurance in Ontario," Budget Paper B, *Ontario Budget 1976*, p. 4. Estimated figures for 1977–1978 indicate further increases to more than $3.1 billion. *Report of the Joint Advisory Committee of the Government of Ontario and the Ontario Medical Association on Methods to Control Health Care Costs* (Toronto: Province of Ontario, December 29, 1977), p. 9.

the consumer price index for all goods and services rose by only 39 percent during the same period.[2] Inflation, therefore, is not the explanation. At the same time, the gross provincial product in Ontario jumped in current dollars by 82 percent. As a result, the share of total provincial output accounted for by insured medical services increased only slightly, from 3.5 percent in 1970–1971 to 3.9 percent in 1975–1976.[3]

Even more important, an increasing proportion of these expenditures has been financed by the Ontario government, with the remainder coming from compulsory consumer premiums and from the federal government. In 1970–1971, the second year of the plan's existence, premiums covered half of total expenditures. With the rise in total cost, the share covered by premiums dropped to 23 percent in 1975–1976. Furthermore, throughout this period, the proportion of total health outlays paid from Ontario's general revenues increased steadily: from only 6 percent in 1970–1971 to nearly 32 percent by 1975–1976.[4] This increasing gap between receipts and expenditures contributed to a growing concern with the cost of providing health care services. Unless changes were made, the health care system would require a continually increasing share of general tax revenues.

The pressure on the Ontario government to limit expenditures was further accentuated by the decision of the federal government to revise its cost-sharing agreements with the provinces. Rather than reimburse without limit a fixed percentage of actual expenditures, it moved on April 1, 1977, to a reimbursement formula related only to population and economic size. Both increased savings and increased costs would henceforth accrue totally to the provincial government.

In these circumstances, the Ontario government searched for ways to reduce costs that would not dismantle the health care system constructed only in 1969. The approach adopted was to limit directly the quantity of services that were supplied. Steps were taken to restrict the number of physicians licensed in Ontario and to limit the quantity of hospital beds in service.

These actions were founded on the presumption that the volume of services provided and financed was directly related to the supply of physicians and hospital beds. When the policy was adopted, the Ontario minister of health maintained explicitly that the number of doctors practicing in the province was a major factor leading to the increase in health care costs. "A doctor costs the system about a

---

[2] *Ontario Budget 1976*, p. 5.
[3] Ibid., p. 4.
[4] Ibid., p. 8.

quarter of a million [dollars] a year," the minister stated. His position was that the larger the number of physicians, the greater the demand for government-financed services.[5]

In making this policy decision, the provincial government relied heavily on a 1974 report by an advisory body to the minister of health.[6] The report concluded:

> There is no evidence to suggest that the standard of health care in Ontario would be significantly improved if large numbers of physicians were added to our medical manpower, yet there is evidence that the number of practicing physicians is one of the prime determinants of health care costs. Steps must be taken to insure that the number of physicians entering practice in the Province does not increase unreasonably or without certain checks and balances.[7]

In arriving at this conclusion, the report relied on the finding that a positive correlation exists between health care costs per capita and the number of doctors per capita.[8]

The program of supply restraint started in 1975. As stated by the minister of health at the time, its objective was to "hold the ratio of doctor to population at one to 585 until 1980."[9] To this end, the influx of physicians from abroad was restricted and medical school enrollments were fixed at existing levels. Professional licensing was used specifically to limit the size of the profession rather than for its original purpose of ensuring that practitioners reach at least minimum standards of professional competence.

The original policy actions concentrated on restricting the number of foreign physicians, a measure which had the greatest political appeal. By the latter part of 1977, however, it became evident that these actions were insufficient and further steps would be needed. Indeed, rather than successfully limiting the relative number of physicians, the government reported that the physician-population ratio had increased slightly to 1 to 560.[10] Moreover, it was predicted at the time that despite existing controls, this ratio would continue to rise and reach 1 to 540 by the early 1980s.[11]

The new minister of health announced, "My predecessor put

[5] *The Globe and Mail* (Toronto), January 16, 1975, p. 1.
[6] *Physician Manpower* (Toronto: Ontario Council of Health, 1974).
[7] Ibid., p. 11.
[8] M.A. Baltzan, "Medical Care Costs and Physician Manpower: A New Economic Theory," *Canadian Medical Association Journal*, vol. 108 (January 6, 1973), pp. 101–111.
[9] Frank S. Miller, "Remarks" (Toronto, October 28, 1975), p. 5.
[10] *The Globe and Mail* (Toronto), October 26, 1977, p. 13.
[11] *Report of the Joint Advisory Committee*, p. 32.

clamps on doctors coming from other countries," but it appeared now that restrictions might have to be placed on the flow of physicians from Quebec.[12] Manpower planning had led inexorably to location controls, even within Canada.

In the case of hospital beds, the policy is similar. Provincial objectives were set originally at 4.0 active treatment beds per 1,000 persons, and 4.5 per 1,000 in northern Ontario. According to the ministry of health, this left 6,000 surplus active treatment beds in Ontario, of which 3,000 were being removed from service.[13] This policy was implemented by reducing the number of beds staffed in ongoing hospitals and by the shutdown of entire hospitals. For the most part, decisions on specific closings were made on an ad hoc basis. The leading candidates for closure were smaller hospitals with alternative facilities within reasonable proximity and hospitals which required rebuilding programs for continued operation. In addition, specific hospital departments have been closed, mergers of hospital facilities encouraged, and hospital spending plans curtailed. In the interests of controlling costs, the provincial government has determined which hospitals will close and which will remain open and the number of hospital beds in service, as well as other operating characteristics. To maintain its program of supply restraint, the provincial government has been forced to accept an ever-growing control over the health care system.

In 1978 budgetary pressures remained tight and further restraint was applied. The minister of health announced that after April 1, 1978, "all new capital projects . . . will be planned on new active treatment bed ratios of 3.5 beds per 1,000 referral population in Southern Ontario, and 4.0 per 1,000 in Northern Ontario."[14] Centralized control increased as the financial burden grew more taut.

Government planning has become an indispensable part of the program of cost control. In characteristic fashion, a 1979 government report maintained that

> At this time the most urgently needed actions include:
> 1. the identification and elimination of excess acute care beds in hospitals;
> 2. the closure or conversion of hospitals or unutilized units;
> 3. the pooling of units across hospitals to reduce duplication of facilities.[15]

---

[12] *The Globe and Mail* (Toronto), October 26, 1977, p. 13.
[13] Frank S. Miller, "Remarks" (Toronto, February 2, 1976).
[14] Dennis Timbrell, *Statement* (Toronto, February 7, 1978), p. 6.
[15] Ontario Economic Council, *Issues and Alternatives, Update 1979* (Toronto, 1979), p. 26.

Detailed examination of physical facilities was required so that specific allocation decisions could be made.

At the same time, however, the report acknowledged that such decisions conflict with "the desire of hospitals for autonomy, for survival, and for expansion and growth, and frequently too the importance of a hospital to the local economy."[16] These decisions invariably are made in a political setting, and it is hardly surprising that several were modified or reversed when they encountered strong opposition.[17] Political forces have become paramount, and this report recognized that existing policies of cost containment "cannot be applied continuously, [as] they have encountered formidable resistance from physicians, hospital administrators, and the public."[18]

All of these measures have followed relentlessly from the original government decision on national health insurance. Indeed, from the vantage point of 1979, the pattern of policy making seems inevitable. One set of government actions creates circumstances that lead directly to new problems that require further measures for solution. In examining this history of policy making, one is struck by Professor Coase's apt statement: "The kind of situation which economists [and others] are prone to consider as requiring corrective government action, is, in fact, often the result of governmental action."[19]

The original decision was to eliminate financial constraints as a factor limiting the demand for medical services. Prices were set generally at zero with the expectation that medical, rather than economic, considerations would determine what care would be provided and to whom. Whatever existing price constraints there were prior to the introduction of national health insurance in Canada were removed.

If financial incentives were not to be used in restraining demand, it became evident that other means were necessary. This conclusion should not have been surprising, for *scarcity* is a fundamental economic proposition. Unless society is willing to devote increasing pro-

---

[16] Ibid., pp. 26–27.
[17] Ibid., p. 25.
[18] Ibid., p. 27.
[19] Ronald H. Coase, "The Problem of Social Cost," *Journal of Law and Economics*, vol. 3 (October 1960), p. 281. Current government policies regarding the appropriate number of hospital beds in Ontario have an especially ironic ring when viewed from a larger perspective. An Ontario Health Survey Report in 1951 set a standard of 5.5 active-treatment beds per 1,000 population as an appropriate goal. By the end of 1954, the provincial ratio was only 4.4 per 1,000, and population increase alone required 800 new beds per year. Policies were clearly required to stimulate hospital construction. The direction of public policy has clearly depended on the arbitrary standard adopted for the "right" number of hospital beds. See Malcolm G. Taylor, *Health Insurance and Canadian Public Policy* (Montreal: McGill Queen's University Press, 1978), chap. 3, especially p. 110.

portions of its resources to the health care sector, some vehicle for imposing restraint is required. What is most interesting about the Ontario experience is that scarcity was ignored in a reliance on medical determinants of the volume of care. Financial constraints were removed, but nothing was put in their place. After a few years, however, it became obvious that something was needed to replace the constraints that had been removed. It is a fact of economic life that *we cannot eliminate scarcity by government decree.* The Ontario experience provides a clear example.

Restraining Demand through Direct Controls

The existing program of direct controls depends crucially on the relationships between the supplies of physicians and of hospital beds and the volume of services provided that were explored in chapter 3. As reported, there is support for existing policy measures within the current structure of the medical care system. Limiting the volume of services will directly reduce total outlays for medical care in Ontario.

In imposing a policy of supply restraint, the distinction must be drawn between the roles of general practitioners and of specialists. As indicated in the empirical analysis, the number of specialists has a major impact on the volume of both physician and hospital services. The number of GPs, on the other hand, has a much smaller effect in both areas. Indeed it was difficult to find significant coefficients to measure these effects. Despite the announced policy of maintaining approximately the current ratio of 45 percent specialists to 55 percent GPs,[20] a smaller proportion of specialists would likely lead to lower outlays on medical care.

A critical question is how much restraint to apply. Beyond what point would the quantity and quality of care be reduced by so much as to jeopardize health standards? An available benchmark is the World Health Organization (WHO) standard, and, whatever its underlying justification, it has been seized upon by the provincial government. According to the WHO, the "ideal" standard for a developed country is the ratio of 1 physician to 650 of the population.

The difference between the 1975 ratio of 1:585 (1.71 per 1,000) and the WHO standard of 1:650 (1.54 per 1,000) is 0.17 physicians per 1,000 of the population, which represents a 10 percent decline from the 1975 ratio. If the entire decline were applied to specialists,

---

[20] Frank S. Miller, "Remarks" (Toronto, October 28, 1975), p. 5.

TABLE 4

REVENUE SAVINGS FROM REDUCED NUMBER OF SPECIALISTS

	Specialists Reduced by 22.7%	Specialists Reduced by 10.0%
Physician services		
Reduced no. of medical claims per capita	0.96	0.42
Revenue savings (millions of dollars)	114	50
Hospital services		
Reduced no. of bed-days per capita	0.173	0.076
Revenue savings (millions of dollars)	160	70

NOTE: The elasticity used for physician services is 0.93, which is derived from equation 4, table 1, and the elasticity used for hospital services is 0.5, which is derived from equation 1, table 3. The resulting predictions of the percentage decline in services provided are deducted from the mean value of the dependent variable in each equation to obtain the figures given for reduced number of medical claims or reduced number of bed-days. These values are then multiplied by the 1975–1976 insured population in Ontario of 8,243,000 and by the average costs per medical claim and per patient-day in 1975–1976 of $14.43 and $112.00, respectively, to obtain the revenue savings figures given.

there would be a 22.7 percent fall in their number. Rather than the current ratio of 44:56 between specialists and GPs, the ratio would decline to 38:62.

In the analysis above, we computed elasticities of both physician and hospital services with respect to the number of specialists. These elasticities are used to estimate the lower expenditures due to an assumed specific reduction in the supply of specialists per capita. As indicated in table 4, savings in both physician and hospital services are estimated at $274 million from a decline in specialists per capita of 22.7 percent, and at $120 million from a decline of 10 percent. These figures represent savings of 11.5 percent and 5.1 percent, respectively, of current expenditures on physician and hospital services.[21] While these results provide only rough orders of magnitude, they suggest that substantial savings may accrue from actions taken to reduce the supply of specialists.

Policy actions dealing with the supply of hospital beds are not independent of those concerning the supply of specialists. As found

[21] In making these estimates, we necessarily assume that the relevant elasticities remain constant at their current levels.

in the analysis of the determinants of acute hospital care, the supply of beds is closely tied to the supply of specialists, making it difficult to obtain satisfactory estimates of the separate effects of each. Actions taken regarding specialists often require that corresponding actions be taken concerning available beds, and there is no indication that existing ratios between specialists and beds should be greatly altered. A reasonable approach would be to match decreases in the number of specialists with similar decreases in available beds.

An Evaluation of Direct Controls

Despite the apparent benefits of imposing direct controls, there are substantial disadvantages as well. The disadvantages, however, are attributable more to the underlying program of national health insurance than to the direct controls that have been grafted onto it. Indeed, the latter follow so directly, and apparently inevitably, from the former that any policy evaluation must deal with both. That some form of direct controls is necessary, given the existing system, is evident, but this conclusion has no implications for our evaluation of the overall decision on which the current system in Ontario rests. All that has been concluded to this point is that when financial constraints are removed, others must be put in their place.

What is essentially at issue are the relative merits of restraining demand by raising prices or by restricting available supplies. The former places individuals at risk for large medical bills and permits the wealthy to purchase more services than the poor. However, only those services would be provided for which the value imputed to them by patients, with the advice of their doctors, exceeds the associated cost. If the volume of medical services provided were to increase, we could at least conclude that it was in accord with consumer preferences. No such conclusion can be drawn under the current system of care in Ontario.

At the zero prices mandated under national health insurance in Ontario, the quantity of specialist services demanded exceeds the quantity supplied, so that a queue or other such rationing mechanism must be used. Indeed, as the number of specialists per capita is limited through a program of direct controls, the gap between demand and supply should increase. One likely result is that specialists will use patient queues to economize on their own time. Patients will be required to wait longer for appointments, as well as in doctors' offices and hospitals. In addition, there will be increased travel costs as patients visit the fewer physicians available. In all these respects, we might expect to find increased time-costs of medical services imposed on the patient population.

Economic efficiency will decline with the increased time that productive members of society spend in receiving medical care. There is an important difference in the efficiency implications of allocating medical care by a money price as compared with a time price. If a money price is used, no resources are consumed by the allocation mechanism, although of course it may have important distributive consequences in placing the wealthier members of the community in a favored position. If a time price is used, on the other hand, the time spent in waiting for services is wasted, despite the element of fairness associated with having all members of society treated equally. While there may be distributive gains in allocating medical services by means of time prices, there are efficiency losses.

To be sure, the increased time price may be only one element of the means used to allocate the available supply of services. The major part of the rationing of these services will probably be made by physicians in determining whom they wish to see. If medical services are rationed according to the interests and judgments of physicians, there are various criteria that could be used. Physicians might decide to allocate their services on the basis of medical interest or in terms of the professional challenge offered by a particular case. To physicians, as to other professionals, the run-of-the-mill case may be far less interesting than the unusual one, and it may therefore receive less medical attention. Scientific interest, however, may have little connection either with the gains in improved health resulting from a given course of treatment or with satisfying consumer preferences.

Other criteria on which physicians might choose to ration their services are various consumer characteristics, such as race, social class, or appearance. Discrimination of this sort may increase in situations where few costs are imposed on a discriminator. In a medical care system where the fees for medical services are fixed and where there is excess demand for these services, discrimination may be relatively costless to physicians.

Finally, and perhaps most likely, physicians might decide to allocate their services on the basis of prospective profitability. It is unlikely that the negotiated fee schedule accurately reflects the relative marginal costs to physicians of the services provided. As a result, the gains from providing one set of services will exceed those from providing another. In choosing among patients, therefore, physicians have an economic incentive to accept those patients who require services that are more profitable, rather than those whose needs are more time-consuming, costly, and less profitable.

Policy makers are inevitably concerned with the effect of their actions on community health, whatever the preferences of individuals. While there is little evidence that increased medical services lead on average to improved health, this issue is sufficiently important to require further consideration. What policy decision would be appropriate if it were found that fewer services and lower costs were associated with poorer health for at least some members of society?

There is no simple answer to this question. The achievement of improved health through the medical care system may be an expensive and inefficient undertaking. And there is no easy answer to the related question of how much society should spend to improve the health of a few. In a private market system without insurance, this question is answered by the amount that individuals are willing to spend. With full government insurance, as in Ontario, there is no similar answer. What remain are political decisions, and a prayer that any impact of fewer services on health will be minor.

By eliminating monetary constraints, the Ontario government has been forced to limit the quantity of physicians and of hospital beds. A policy of supply restraint has been adopted that rests on arbitrary standards and requires direct controls. Government officials have come to make even minor decisions regarding the type and quantity of services provided, how they shall be produced, and by whom, as well as who shall receive them. Whether intended or not, this has been the ultimate consequence of the original policy decision.

On the other hand, there assuredly is a gain to most consumers from avoiding the risk of bearing the high costs associated with serious illness; this gain is realized in Ontario. Any evaluation of the Ontario health care system must incorporate these benefits along with the evident disadvantages. Whether such benefits can be obtained without the associated costs is the critical question for health care policy in the United States.

It is apparent that a program of full national health insurance has imposed substantial costs on the province of Ontario. These costs have recently been acknowledged, and there appears to be some retreat from an original position advocating the elimination of all financial constraints on consumers. An advisory report published in the last days of 1977 recommended (1) "that subscribers be charged a substantial amount for the first day of each hospital admission up to a maximum of two days per calendar year," and (2) "that there be no expansion of insured services in any area without rigorous screening . . . [and] that the possibility of reducing the existing list of insured services . . . be given serious consideration."[22] These recommendations may represent a first step away from a commitment to total government health insurance.

---

[22] *Report of the Joint Advisory Committee*, pp. 27, 38.

Implications for the United States

There are many similarities in both the demand and the supply of medical services between the United States and Canada. These parallels can also be applied to Ontario, the most populous of the Canadian provinces. Patients generally expect the same quality of care and have comparable incomes with which to pay for it. Physicians have been trained in similar institutions and appear ready to supply their services in much the same manner as their counterparts in the United States. The differences between the two systems arise largely from the Canadian program of national health insurance.

The primary impact of this program has been to eliminate all financial constraints on the demand for medical services. As should have been anticipated, the quantity of services demanded increased so that the government was forced to impose an alternative set of constraints. The law of scarcity is not so easily repealed. A similar pattern of policy making would probably have the same consequences in the United States.

The most important feature of the system of health insurance in Ontario is *not* that it is administered by the provincial government, nor that it is generally compulsory for all residents of Ontario. What is more important is that the link between who pays the bills and who receives the services has been broken; that the price to consumers at the time their decisions regarding health care are made is effectively zero. To a large extent, this applies as well to many health insurance plans in the United States. Indeed, the fact that consumers have already paid a premium for health insurance does not restrain their demand for services and may even tend to increase it so that they will "get their money's worth."

It is well known that health insurance may lead to an excessive demand for medical services.[23] Whether insurance is provided by the government or by private firms has more to do with how the cost of insurance is financed. An additional factor, however, makes this distinction important. While private insurance carriers may be content to permit increased medical costs to be translated into higher premiums, since this could lead to an increase in profits as well, politicians are generally reluctant to raise taxes accordingly, since their rewards are associated with lower taxes.

As government officials have greater authority over costs of medical care, pressures to constrain these costs may be greater when health insurance is paid by the government rather than by private

---

[23] Mark V. Pauly, *Medical Care at Public Expense* (New York: Praeger, 1971).

insurance companies. These pressures can be expected to lead to increased controls, such as those adopted in Ontario. Although U.S. controls would probably differ from those in Canada, control of some type or other can be expected—if not immediately, at least after a period of time.

With health insurance provided under government auspices and financed from tax revenues, one would expect to find greater pressures to limit costs, which in turn should influence how medicine is organized, as well as the level of fees that are paid. With the Ontario experience as a guide, a change from private to government-financed health insurance in the United States could lead to more controls and lower health costs.

What is clearly required is that insurance, whether provided by a government agency or through private carriers, cover the often very large costs of serious illness. The gains to consumers from risk spreading in this area are likely to be substantial. Professor Feldstein has suggested that insurance benefits be such that out-of-pocket medical costs cannot exceed 10 percent of a family's yearly income.[24] The adoption of this type of sliding scale might require government participation, since payments would start at lower absolute levels for poorer than for wealthier families. Whether through this type of plan or through some other, insurance for catastrophic illness and its associated costs is surely necessary.

Full coverage of all medical expenses as found in Ontario and in many insurance plans in the United States, however, leads directly to an excessive consumption of medical services. Moreover, there are few offsetting benefits from risk spreading since most families require some amount of care during the year. If mandatory health insurance coverage is deemed necessary, it should be combined with the extensive application of coinsurance and deductibles.[25]

The type of complete government-provided health insurance found in Ontario leads inexorably to the imposition of government controls over the size and character of the health care system. While costs may be reduced in this manner, the extensive controls required

---

[24] Martin S. Feldstein, "Hospital Cost Inflation and National Health Insurance," Carl Snyder Memorial Lecture, University of California, Santa Barbara, January 18, 1977, pp. 21–27.
[25] A more complete discussion of these issues can be found in various articles by Professor Feldstein. See Martin S. Feldstein, "The High Cost of Hospitals and What to Do about It," *Public Interest*, no. 48 (Summer 1977), pp. 40–54; and "A New Approach to National Health Insurance," *Public Interest*, no. 23 (Spring 1971), pp. 93–105. For a polemical statement opposing this approach, see M.L. Barer, R.G. Evans, and G.L. Stoddart, *Controlling Health Care Costs by Direct Charges to Patients: Snare or Delusion?* (Toronto: Ontario Economic Council, 1979).

make it not a model to be followed in the United States.[26] By learning from the experience of others, we have the opportunity to fashion a medical care system which rests, to the maximum extent possible, on the wishes and preferences of the American people.

---

[26] It is striking that a recent study of the Canadian health care system recommends various changes more in line with the U.S. system. See A. Blomquist, *The Health Care Business* (Vancouver: The Fraser Institute, 1979).

APPENDIX

Variables Used in Statistical Analysis

1. Quantity of Physicians' Services Provided per Capita

Number of medical claims paid, times the ratio of the average cost per claim in the particular district for the year to the average cost per claim for all districts in the same year; all divided by district population.

From: *Statistical Report on OHIP Medical Experience, 1974–1975,* table 7 and table 12; *1972–1973,* table 7; *OHIP Practitioner Care Statistics, 1973–1974,* table 5.

2. No. of General Practitioners per Capita

Number of GPs divided by district population.

From: *Statistical Report on OHIP Medical Experience, 1974–1975,* table 13.

3. No. of Specialists per Capita

Number of specialists divided by district population.

From: *Statistical Report on OHIP Medical Experience, 1974–1975,* table 13.

4. Total Population in District

From: *Statistical Report on OHIP Medical Experience, 1974–1975,* table 12.

51

5. Population Density in District

From: *Statistical Report on OHIP Medical Experience, 1974–1975,* table 12.

6. Medical School in District

Dummy variable for London, Toronto, Hamilton, Ottawa, Kingston.

7. Proportion of District Population in Urban Areas

1971 district population living in urban areas divided by total population.

From: *1971 Census of Canada,* Catalogue 92–709, table 11.

8. Proportion of District Population of Children

1971 district population of children in families divided by total population.

From: *1971 Census of Canada,* Catalogue 92–709, table 11; and Catalogue 93–715, table 15.

9. Proportion of District Population Female

1971 district population female divided by total population.

From: *1971 Census of Canada,* Catalogue 92–709, table 11.

10. Proportion of District Population over 65

1971 district population in age categories over 65 years divided by total population.

From: *1971 Census of Canada,* Catalogue 92–709, table 11; and Catalogue 92–715, table 9.

11. Average Family Income

1971 average total income of families.

From: *1971 Census of Canada,* Catalogue 93–746, table 3.

12. Quantity of Acute Hospital Services Provided per Capita

Number of bed-days of acute care in public general hospitals, times the ratio of average net allowable standard ward costs per diem in the district and year to the average for all districts for the year, divided by district population.

From: Unpublished data compiled and provided by Data Development and Evaluation Branch, Ministry of Health, Ontario; and *Hospital Statistics, 1972*, table 17; *1973*, table 17; *1974*, table 16.

13. Quantity of Chronic Hospital Services Provided per Capita

Number of bed-days of chronic care provided in general rehabilitation, special rehabilitation, and chronic units in public general hospitals and in public chronic hospitals, times the ratio of average net allowable standard ward costs per diem in the district and year to the average for all districts for the year, divided by district population.

From: *Hospital Statistics, 1972*, tables 3 and 17; *1973*, tables 4 and 17; *1974*, tables 3 and 16.

14. Number of Active Beds Staffed per Capita

Average number of active beds staffed in public general hospitals in district at start and end of year, divided by district population.

From: *Hospital Statistics, 1971*, table 2; *1972*, table 2; *1973*, table 2; *1974*, table 3.

15. Number of Chronic Beds Staffed per Capita

Average number of beds staffed in general rehabilitation, special rehabilitation, and chronic units in public general hospitals and in public chronic hospitals in district at start and end of year, divided by district population.

From: *Hospital Statistics, 1971*, table 2; *1972*, table 2; *1973*, table 2; *1974*, table 3.

16. Number of Hospital Nurses Employed per Capita

Number of full-time nurses employed in public general hospitals in district, divided by district population.

From: Unpublished data compiled and provided by Data Development and Evaluation Branch, Ministry of Health, Ontario.

17. Number of Registered Nurses per Capita

Number of nurses registered in district divided by district population.

From: Unpublished data provided by Health Manpower Planning Section, Ministry of Health, Ontario.

BIBLIOGRAPHY

Acton, Jon Paul. "Nonmonetary Factors in the Demand for Medical Services: Some Empirical Evidence." *Journal of Political Economy* 83, June 1975.

Andreopoulos, Spyros. "The Health of Canadians." *National Health Insurance: Can We Learn from Canada?* Spyros Andreopoulos, ed. New York: Wiley, 1975.

Auster, Richard, et al. "The Production of Health, An Exploratory Study." *Journal of Human Resources* 4, Fall 1969.

Baltzan, M.A. "Medical Care Costs and Physician Manpower: A New Economic Theory." *Canadian Medical Association Journal* 108, January 6, 1973. Reprinted in Ontario Council of Health. *Physician Manpower.* Toronto, 1974.

Barer, M.L., R.G. Evans, and G.L. Stoddart. *Controlling Health Care Costs by Direct Charges to Patients: Snare or Delusion?* Toronto: Ontario Economic Council, 1979.

Beck, R.G. "The Effects of Co-payment on the Poor." *Journal of Human Resources* 9, March 1974.

Benham, L., A. Maurizi, and M.W. Reder. "Migration, Location and Remuneration of Medical Personnel: Physicians and Dentists." *Review of Economics and Statistics* 50, August 1968.

Berki, Seymour. *Hospital Economics.* Lexington, Mass.: D.C. Heath, 1972.

Blomquist, A. *The Health Care Business.* Vancouver: The Fraser Institute, 1979.

Brown, M., A. Benham, and L. Benham. "The Introduction of Medicare in Canada and Windfall Gains to Physicians." Unpublished paper, October 1976.

Bunker, John P., and Bryan W. Brown. "The Physician-Patient as an Informed Consumer of Surgical Services." *New England Journal of Medicine* 290, May 9, 1974.

Census of Canada, 1971. Ottawa.

Coase, Ronald H. "The Problem of Social Cost." *Journal of Law and Economics* 3, October 1960.

Enterline, Philip E., et al. "Effects of 'Free' Medical Care on Medical Practice—The Quebec Experience." *New England Journal of Medicine* 288, May 31, 1973.

———. "Physicians' Working Hours and Patients Seen before and after National Health Insurance." *Medical Care* 12, February 1975.

———. "The Distribution of Medical Services before and after 'Free' Medical Care—The Quebec Experience." *New England Journal of Medicine* 289, November 29, 1973.

Evans, Robert G. *Price Formation in the Market for Physician Services.* Ottawa: Price and Income Commission, 1972.

———. "Supplier-Induced Demand: Some Empirical Evidence and Implications." *The Economics of Health and Medical Care.* Mark Perlman, ed. New York: Wiley, 1974.

———. "Beyond the Medical Marketplace: Expenditure, Utilization and Pricing of Insured Health in Canada." *National Health Insurance: Can We Learn From Canada?* Spyros Andreopoulos, ed. New York: Wiley, 1975.

———. "Does Canada Have Too Many Doctors?—Why Nobody Loves an Immigrant Physician." *Canadian Public Policy* 2, Spring 1976.

———. "Does Canada Have Too Many Doctors?—Two Views." *Canadian Public Policy* 3, Summer 1967.

Evans, Robert G., E.N.A. Parish, and Floyd Sully. "Medical Productivity, Scale Effects, and Demand Generation." *Canadian Journal of Economics* 6, August 1973.

Evans, Robert G., and M.F. Williamson. *Extending Canadian Health Insurance.* Toronto: University of Toronto Press, 1978.

Feldstein, Martin S. "A New Approach to National Health Insurance." *Public Interest* 23, Spring 1971.

———. "Hospital Cost Inflation." *American Economic Review* 61, December 1971.

———. "Hospital Cost Inflation and National Health Insurance." Carl Snyder Memorial Lecture, University of California, Santa Barbara, January 18, 1977.

———. "The High Cost of Hospitals—and What to Do about It." *Public Interest* 48, Summer 1977.

———. "The Rising Price of Physicians' Services." *Review of Economics and Statistics* 52, May 1970.

———. "The Welfare Loss of Excess Health Insurance." *Journal of Political Economy* 81, March 1973.

———. "Econometric Studies of Health Economics." *Frontiers in Quantitative Economics.* Michael D. Intriligator and David Kendrick, eds. Amsterdam: North Holland, 1974.

Fraser, R.D. *Health Economics Symposium, Proceedings of the First Canadian Conference.* Queens University, Kingston, Ontario, 1976.

———. *Selected Economic Aspects of the Health Care Sector in Ontario.* Toronto: Province of Ontario, 1970.

Fuchs, Victor R. "Some Economic Aspects of Mortality in Developed Countries." *The Economics of Health and Medical Care.* Mark Perlman, ed. New York: Wiley, 1974.

―――. *Who Shall Live?* New York: Basic Books, 1974.

Fuchs, Victor R., and Marcia J. Kramer. *Determinants of Expenditures for Physicians' Services in the United States, 1948–1968.* Washington, D.C.: National Center for Health Services Research and Development, Department of Health, Education, and Welfare, 1972.

Lalonde, Marc. *A New Perspective on the Health of Canadians.* Ottawa, 1974.

Leclair, Maurice. "The Canadian Health Care System." *National Health Insurance: Can We Learn from Canada?* Spyros Andreopoulos, ed. New York: Wiley, 1975.

Lerner, Monroe. "Conceptualization of Health and Social Wellbeing." *Health Status Indexes.* Robert L. Berg, ed. Chicago: Hospital Research and Educational Trust, 1973.

Migue, J.L., and G. Belanger. *The Price of Health.* Toronto: Macmillan, 1974.

Miller, Frank S. "Remarks." Toronto, October 28, 1975.

―――. "Remarks." Toronto, February 2, 1976.

Ministry of Health, Province of Ontario. *Constraints Program Review, January–February 1976.* Toronto, March 5, 1976.

―――. *Statistical Report on OHIP Medical Experience, 1972–1973.* Toronto.

―――. *Hospital Statistics, 1973.* Toronto.

―――. *OHIP Practitioner Care Statistics, 1973–1974.* Toronto.

―――. *Statistical Report on OHIP Medical Experience.* Toronto, June 1975.

Newhouse, Joseph P. "Towards a Theory of Nonprofit Institutions: An Economic Model of a Hospital." *American Economics Review* 60, March 1970.

Newhouse, Joseph P., and Charles E. Phelps. "Price and Income Elasticities for Medical Care Services." *The Economics of Health and Medical Care.* Mark Perlman, ed. New York: Wiley, 1973.

Office of the Registrar General, Province of Ontario. *Vital Statistics for 1972.* Toronto.

―――. *Vital Statistics for 1973.* Toronto.

Ontario Budget 1976. Toronto.

Ontario Council of Health. *Physician Manpower.* Toronto, 1974.

Ontario Economic Council. *Issues and Alternatives: Update 1979.* Toronto, 1979.

Ontario Statistical Review. 1973.

Pauly, Mark V. *Medical Care at Public Expense.* New York: Praeger, 1971.

―――. "The Role of Demand Creation in the Provision of Health Services." Unpublished paper presented at meetings of the American Economic Association, Dallas, Texas, December 30, 1975.

Rosett, Richard N., and Lien-fu Huang. "The Effect of Health Insurance on the Demand for Medical Care." *Journal of Political Economy* 81, March 1973.

Rafferty, John, ed. *Health Manpower and Productivity.* Lexington: Heath, 1974.

Reinhardt, Uwe E. *Physician Productivity and the Demand for Health Manpower.* Cambridge, Mass.: Ballinger, 1975.

Report of the Joint Advisory Committee of the Government of Ontario and the Ontario Medical Association on Methods to Control Health Care Costs. Toronto: Province of Ontario, December 29, 1977.

Ruderman, A. Peter. "The Economic Position of Ontario Physicians and the Relation between the Schedule of Fees and Actual Income from Fee Practice." *Special Study Regarding the Medical Profession in Ontario, A Report to the Ontario Medical Association.* Edward A. Pickering. April 1973 (Pickering Report).

———. "The Political Economy of Fee-Setting and the Future of Fee-for-Service." R.D. Fraser, ed. *Health Economics Symposium, Proceedings of the First Canadian Conference.* Kingston, Ontario: Queens University, 1976.

Sloan, Frank A. "Physician Supply Behavior in the Short Run." *Industrial and Labor Relations Review* 28, July 1975.

Taylor, Malcolm G. *Health Insurance and Canadian Public Policy.* Montreal: McGill-Queens University Press, 1978, chap. 3.

The Globe and Mail. Toronto, January 16, 1975.

The Globe and Mail. Toronto, October 26, 1977.

Timbrell, Dennis. *Statement.* Toronto, February 7, 1978.

Zeckhauser, Richard. "Medical Insurance: A Case Study of the Trade-Off between Risk Spreading and Appropriate Incentives." *Journal of Economic Theory* 2, March 1970.

www.ingramcontent.com/pod-product-compliance
Lightning Source LLC
Jackson TN
JSHW011943131224
75386JS00041B/1538

* 9 7 8 0 8 4 4 7 3 3 7 9 1 *